COLUMBIA ENGLISH GRAMMAR for ACT

WITH ANSWERS

A SCORE-RAISING ACT GRAMMAR BOOK FOR ADVANCED STUDENTS

Richard Lee, Ph.D.

COLUMBIA PRESS

Copyright © 2012 by Richard Lee, Columbia Press

All rights reserved.

No part of this book may be reproduced or distributed in any form or by any means without the written permission of the copyright owner.

All inquiries should be addressed to:

COLUMBIA PRESS

207-1089 West Broadway

Vancouver, BC V6H 1E5

Website: www.cpwise.com

Email: richardleephd@hotmail.com

ISBN-13: 978-1-927647-02-8

To Nancy, Philip, and Christina

CONTENTS

TO THE STUDENT

Verb Tenses

1. Errors with the Simple Past Tense and the Present Perfect Tense 11
2. Errors with Present Perfect Tense and the Past Perfect Tense 15
3. Use the Correct Tense with *Time Expressions* 18

Verbals and Modal Verbs

4. Errors with Verbals 21
5. Errors with Modal Verbs 26

Dangling Modifiers and Misplaced Modifiers

6. Errors with Dangling Modifiers 31
7. Misplaced Modifiers: Position Adjectives and Adverbs Correctly 34

Parallel Structures

8. Errors with Parallel Structure with Coordinate Conjunctions 37
9. Errors with Parallel Structure with Correlative Conjunctions 40
10. Errors with Parallel Structure with Comparisons 43

Sujbect-Verb Agreement

11 Faulty Subject-Verb Agreement: Subject with Appositive and Verb   46
12 Faulty Subject-Verb Agreement: Indefinite Subject and Verb   49
13 Faulty Subject-Verb Agreement: Collective Subject and Verb   53

Noun Clauses

14 Errors with Noun Clauses   57
15 Use Noun Clause *Connector/Subject* Correctly   61
16 Use Noun Clause *Connector/Object* Correctly   64

Adjective Clauses (Relative Clauses)

17 Errors with Adjective Clauses   67
18 Errors with Adjective Clause Markers   70

Adverb Clauses (Adverbial Clauses)

19 Use Adverb *Time* and *Cause Markers* Correctly   73
20 Use Adverb *Contrast*, *Condition*, *Manner*, and *Place Markers* Correctly   76
21 Use Adverb *Cause-and-Result Markers* Correctly   80

Conditionals (Subjunctive Mood)

22 Errors with Conditionals: Impossible Situation in the Present Time   83
23 Errors with Conditionals: Impossible Situation in the Past Time   86

Passive Voice

24 Errors with Passive Voice   89

Nouns

25 Errors with Nouns   92

Pronouns

26 Errors with Pronouns   96
27 Errors with Reflexive Pronouns   99
28 Errors with Pronoun References   102

Adjectives and Adverbs

29 Errors with Adjectives and Adverbs   105
30 Errors with Comparatives and Superlatives   108

Articles

31 Errors with Articles   112

Prepositions

32 Errors with Prepositions   115

ANSWER KEY   121

INDEX   139

ACKNOWLEDGMENTS   149

ABOUT THE AUTHOR   151

TO THE STUDENT

COLUMBIA ENGLISH GRAMMAR FOR ACT is written specifically for students who are preparing to take the ACT test. It has 32 score-raising lessons covering all the absolutely essential grammar rules, such as *subject-verb agreement*, *dangling modifier*, *parallel structure*, and others which are most often tested on the ACT.

To help you understand better and memorize these key grammar rules more easily, all the lessons are designed to follow the same format with the following outstanding features:

- **ERROR EXAMPLES:** show you what kinds of mistakes most often made at ACT and how to correct them;

- **GRAMMAR RULES:** teach you all the grammar testing points you need to know to help you ace the test;

- **PRACTICE TESTS:** Use sample *Sentence Correction* and *Sentence Completion* questions to help you memorize these grammar rules through repetition;

- **ANSWER KEYS:** provide answers and explanations to help you avoid the mistakes forever.

COLUMBIA ENGLISH GRAMMAR FOR ACT gives you an English professor's proven method, guaranteed to help you master all the essential grammar rules for the test. If you can spend about 15 minutes a day on each lesson, it will definitely help raise your ACT score, and, in the mean time, you will become a much better reader and writer.

Richard Lee, Ph.D.
December 2013

Lesson 1

ERRORS WITH THE SIMPLE PAST TENSE AND THE PRESENT PERFECT TENSE

ERROR EXAMPLE

    WRONG: Americans found themselves with less free time over the past few decades even though they are earning more money.

    RIGHT: Americans **have found** themselves with less free time over the past few decades even though they are earning more money.

GRAMMAR RULES

The most common verb tense mistakes we make are our confusion of and the incorrect use of the Simple Past Tense and the Present Perfect Tense.

1. THE SIMPLE PAST TENSE

We use the Simple Past Tense to express an event or situation that began and ended in the past.

    WRONG: We have moved to New York City in 1989.

    RIGHT: We **moved** to New York City in 1989.

2. THE PRESENT PERFECT TENSE

We use the Present Perfect Tense to give the idea that the action started in the past and still relates to the present. In other words, the action in the past has a result now.

> WRONG: Philip have lived in Denver for ten years before he moved to the Silicon Valley to start his own company.

> RIGHT: Philip **had lived** in Denver for ten years before he moved to the Silicon Valley to start his own company.

The meaning of a verb tense in a sentence must agree with the time meaning of the rest of the sentence. The time meaning of a sentence is often determined by words or expressions which we call *time markers*.

The following are some of the most commonly used *TIME MARKERS*:

1. SINCE

We use *since* with the perfect tenses to indicate a particular time.

> Because National statistics on crime **have** only **been kept** *since* 1930, it is impossible to make judgments about crime during the early years of the nation.

2. FOR

We use *for* with the perfect tenses or the simple tenses to indicate a duration of time.

> She **has been** in the U.S. *for* six months.

3. YET

We use *yet* with the perfect tenses in negative meanings and in questions.

> I have just got my acceptance letter from Yale University. **Have** you **heard** from Harvard University *yet*?

4. ALREADY

We use *already* with the perfect tenses in affirmative meanings.

> By the time I **got** to the airport, the plane **had** *already* **taken off**.

5. DURING

We use *during* with the simple and continuous tenses to show a duration of time. It is not usually used with the perfect tenses.

> Everybody **is having** a hard time *during* the recession.

PRACTICE TESTS

Test 1. SENTENCE COMPLETION: Choose the CORRECT answer.

1. By September 2018, Jack Morgan will_____.

   A. graduate from Harvard Law School

   B. have graduated from Harvard Law School

2. In 2012, Clarissa_____Chairman of the Women's Rights International.

   A. had become

   B. became

3. These kinds of clothes_____ very popular in the countryside during the depression.

   A. were

   B. have been

4. When you called me last night, I_____ dinner with my parents.

   A. was having

   B. had had

5. They _____.five skyscrapers in Star City by the end of 2011.

   A. already built.

   B. had already built

Test 2. SENTENCE CORRECTION: Choose the INCORRECT word or phrase and CORRECT it.

1. By the time I got to the airport, the plane has already taken off.

2. I traveled to five major cities since I cam to the United States last year.

3. The ground is wet. It must rained.

4. I took a shower when Helen called me last night.

5. By the end of 2005 I have already finished my bachelor's degree in computer science at the University of Rochester.

Lesson 2

ERRORS WITH THE PRESENT PERFECT TENSE AND THE PAST PERFECT TENSE

ERROR EXAMPLE

>WRONG: After the votes were counted, it had been determined that Obama was the winner.

>RIGHT: After the votes **had been counted**, it **was** determined that Obama was the winner.

GRAMMAR RULES

The Present Perfect Tense (*have* + past participle) and the Past Perfect Tense (*had* + past participle) are often confused. They have completely different uses, and we should learn how to differentiate them.

1.THE PRESENT PERFECT TENSE: *HAVE* + PAST PARTICIPLE

The Present Perfect Tense refers to an action or situation that started in the past and still relates to the present.

>I **have** just **finished** reading the novel this morning.

>Michael **has been** busy with his term papers all week.

>WRONG: By the time we got to the party, the guests have already left.

>RIGHT: By the time we got to the party, the guests **had** already **left**.

2. THE PAST PERFECT TENSE: *HAD* + PAST PARTICIPLE

The Past Perfect Tense refers to an activity or situation that took place before another past activity or situation.

The City of Shanghai **had** already **built** more than three hundred skyscrapers by the end of 2008.

When we got to the station, the train **had** just **left** for Atlanta.

WRONG: I had taken five courses in computer science since I came to New York University last year.

RIGHT: I **have taken** five courses in computer science since I came to New York University last year.

PRACTICE TESTS

Test 1. SENTENCE COMPLETION: Choose the CORRECT answer.

1. When I got home from school, my parents_____.

   A. went to sleep

   B. had gone to sleep

2. I don't know If you _____ from University of Washington yet.

   A. had heard

   B. have heard

3. The train_____ the station for Atlantic City.

   A. has just left

   B. had just left

4. By two o'clock this morning, Mary _____ eighteen hours continuously without any stop.

   A. worked
   B. had worked

5. Great changes_____ in the rural area since the new economic reform.

A. had taken place

B. have taken place

Test 2. SENTENCE CORRECTION: Choose the INCORRECT word or phrase and CORRECT it.

1. After I complete my studies in America, I will return to my own country.

2. When Jennifer began her schooling, she has already memorized more than 500 new words.

3. Since I am grown up now, I should help my parents in finances.

4. Up to now, the city had built five community centres.

5. By the end of 1988, the number of international students in the country risen to two million.

Lesson 3

USE THE CORRECT TENSE WITH *TIME EXPRESSIONS*

ERROR EXAMPLE

>WRONG: The Senate votes on the law to ban cigarette smoking in public in 1990.
>
>RIGHT: The Senate **voted** on the law to ban cigarette smoking in public *in* 1990.

GRAMMAR RULES

To be able to use *TIME EXPRESSIONS* correctly is fairly important; for a *TIME EXPRESSION* clearly indicates what kind of verb tense is needed in the sentence.

>*So far* we **have done** what we could to help these homeless people.
>
>The children **had** already **gone** to sleep *by the time* we got home last night.
>
>WRONG: Joy is very busy *lately*.
>
>RIGHT: Joy **has been** very busy *lately*.

THE MOST COMMONLY USED *TIME EXPRESSIONS*:

1. **We use the following words or phrases of time with the Present Perfect Tense.**

    a) *for* and *since*: We use *for* and *since* to say *how long*.

    I **have been** in New York City *for twenty years.*

She **has known** George *since 1999*.

b) ***recently, in the last few days, so far:*** We use *recently, in the last few days, so far* etc. to indicate a period that continues until now.

I **have not seen** Bill *recently*.

She **has met** with a lot of people *in the last few days*.

George **has completed** two novels *so far* this year.

c) ***today, this morning/week/month/year***: We use *time adverbs* that refer to the present, such as *today, this morning/ week/ month/ year* etc.

We **have not received** the newspaper *today*.

The city **has built** a new stadium *this year*.

d) ***just, already, yet:*** We normally use *just, already*, *yet* with Present Perfect Tense.

Have you **had** your dinner *yet*?

She **has** *already* **made** a lot of new friends in America since she came last month.

WRONG: We had *just* seen the new movie.

RIGHT: We **have** *just* **seen** the new movie.

2. *By + time (past)*: **We use *by + time (past)* with Past Perfect Tense.**

WRONG: By the turn of the century, computers have become very popular in the developing countries.

RIGHT: *By the turn of the century*, computers **had become** very popular in the developing countries.

PRACTICE TESTS

Test 1. SENTENCE COMPLETION: Choose the CORRECT answer.

1. People's lives_____better and better ever since the country won its independence.

A. have become

B. had become

2. Forks and spoons_____ by the people in the West for centuries.

   A. are used

   B. have been used

3. He_____ to more than fifty countries in the last few years.

   A. has traveled

   B. traveled

4. The little girl_____ very strangely lately.

   A. had behaved

   B. has behaved

5. We_____ more than twenty-five new employees so far.

   A. have recruited

   B. recruited

Test 2. SENTENCE CORRECTION: Choose the INCORRECT word or phrase and CORRECT it.

1. Have you talked to the Department Chair already?

2. Jenny had never had lobsters before.

3. He is waiting for you for a long time.

4. Since 1979 great changes took place in my hometown.

5. By 2006 our city has built more than thirty public libraries.

Lesson 4

ERRORS WITH VERBALS

ERROR EXAMPLE

> WRONG: It was the task of all interesting nations to make sure this new state of affairs did not spill over into tension or worse.
>
> RIGHT: It was the task of all **interested** nations to make sure this new state of affairs did not spill over into tension or worse.

GRAMMAR RULES

Verbals are participles, gerunds, and infinitives. The following are the various kinds of uses of verbals:

1. PARTICIPLES can be used as adjectives. For present participles, they end with *–ing*; for past participles, they end with *–ed*. When modifying nouns, present participles tend to have active meaning whereas past participles have passive meaning.

> She is rumoured to be a **living** dictionary. (Present Participle)
>
> The **damaged** car was finally repaired. (Past Participle)
>
> WRONG: The millionaire's stealing Land Rover was finally recovered with the help of the police.

RIGHT: The millionaire's **stolen** Land Rover was finally recovered with the help of the police.

WRONG: The woman put the cleaning cups on the table.

RIGHT: The woman put the **cleaned** cups on the table.

2. GERUNDS are verbal nouns. They end in *–ing* like the present participle. They can be used as the subjects of verbs, the objects of prepositions and verbs like the following:

admit	*deny*	*postpone*
appreciate	*enjoy*	*practice*
avoid	*finish*	*stop*
cannot help	*keep*	*suggest*
consider		

She has finished **reading** all the required books for the exam.

You must avoid **making** this kind of mistakes again.

Mary really enjoyed **meeting** her new roommates.

WRONG: Young people should always look forward to see miracles happen in their lives.

RIGHT: Young people should always look forward to **seeing** miracles happen in their lives.

WRONG: Jack denied to commit the crime.

RIGHT: Jack denied **committing** the crime.

The following verb phrases (verb + prepositions) can be followed by the gerund (V + ing):

be accustomed to	*decide on*	*plan on*
be interested in	*get through*	*put off*
be opposed to	*keep on*	*think about*
be used to	*look forward to*	*think of*

She was used to **living** in the country

We are looking forward to **seeing** you in Dallas.

If you keep on **practicing,** you will get a higher score on the exam.

I am thinking of **going** back to Paris after graduation.

3. **INFINITIVES are formed with** *to* **plus the simple form of the verb. They can be used as the subjects of verbs and the objects of verbs like the following:**

agree	*forbid*	*mean*
care	*forget*	*offer*
decide	*hope*	*plan*
deserve	*intend*	*pretend*
fail	*learn*	*refuse*

He has agreed **to go** swimming with me.

We intend **to hold** the biggest celebration party ever.

Mary failed **to attend** the seminar on Saturday.

The secretary offered **to come** in early.

WRONG: John Glenn was the first American orbiting the Earth.

RIGHT: John Glenn was the first American **to orbit** the Earth.

WRONG: She has agreed to consider to quit smoking.

RIGHT: She has agreed to consider **quitting** smoking.

PRACTICE TESTS

Test 1. SENTENCE COMPLETION: Choose the CORRECT answer.

1. The _____ basketball players were too tired to move after they had won the championship.

   A. exhausting

   B. exhausted

2. Tenants of this building are advised to shut the windows in winter; for we_____.

   A. cannot afford heating the outside

   B. cannot afford to heat the outside

3. Nobody can avoid_____ in the United States.

   A. to be taxed

   B. being taxed

4. Unfortunately, Mary failed_____ to the convocation on time.

   A. coming

   B. to come

5. Michael definitely deserved_____a raise this year.

   A. to get

   B. getting

Test 2. SENTENCE CORRECTION: Choose the INCORRECT word or phrase and CORRECT it.

1. This new sports car is very easy driving.

2. The most important discovery knowing to all might be DNA.

3. No rich person can afford feeding such a hungry nation after the war.

4. Have finished dinner, we took a walk along the Thames.

5. No one looks forward to hear bad news after the college entrance exam.

Lesson 5

ERRORS WITH MODAL VERBS

ERROR EXAMPLE

    WRONG: All of the books that you will need for this report can found in the library.

    RIGHT: All of the books that you will need for this report **can be found** in the library.

GRAMMAR RULES

The modal auxiliaries in English are *can, could, had better, may, might, must, ought (to), shall, should, will, would.*

In general, modals express that a speaker feels something is necessary, advisable, permissible, possible, or probable.

The following outlines the uses of verb forms after modals:

1. After all MODALS use the base form of the verb (V)

    Henry **must go** to New York this weekend.

    She **should pay** more attention to his research project.

    We **had better leave** early so that we can catch the flight.

    You **will have** to get this done by five o'clock this afternoon.

We **may choose** to write this exam in class or at home.

He **might come** to New York next week.

WRONG: According to Samson, his dog can recognizes English words.

RIGHT: According to Samson, his dog **can recognize** English words.

WRONG: She had better to get prepared for her final examination.

RIGHT: She **had better get** prepared for her final examination.

WRONG: If he had followed my advice, he wouldn't gone to a foreign country to find a job.

RIGHT: If he had followed my advice, he **wouldn't have gone** to a foreign country to find a job.

2. Use the Past Participle after MODAL + HAVE

I **should have** *applied* to Harvard University earlier.

She **must have** *got* his test result for the TOEFL.

Tom and Jessie **might have** *enjoyed* the party.

3. When we change direct speech to indirect speech, *could, would, should,* and *might* do not change form.

Direct Speech:

"You **should** always finish your homework on time."

Indirect Speech:

My supervisor said that **I should** always finish my homework on time.

4. Use *MUST HAVE* + Past Participle for past conclusion only

The ground is wet, it **must have rained**.

It's almost midnight; Mary **must have gone** to sleep.

5. Use *HAD* + Infinitive for past obligation

She **had to go** to see the doctor last night.

When we were poor, we **had to eat** grass in order to survive.

6. The MODAL *WOULD* is often combined with *like to* or *rather* to form a modal-like verb. Use *WOULD LIKE TO* to mean *want to*; use *WOULD RATHER* to mean *prefer to*:

I **would like to** go to the movie tonight.

I **would rather** go to the movie tonight than go to a party.

7. MODALS used in passive sentences must be followed by *be* + *Past Participle* of the main verb

The woman who **could** *be identified* by her finger print was arrested for theft at the airport.

The boy who **might** *be punished* for not doing his homework is actually a very good friend of mine.

PRACTICE TESTS

Test 1. SENTENCE COMPLETION: Choose the CORRECT answer.

1. The bathroom is flooding. The pipes must_____.

   A. be broken

   B. have been broken

2. It_____ last night because the ground is wet.

   A. rained

   B. must have rained

3. It is almost two o'clock in the morning. They must _____ in New York.

   A. have arrived

   B. arrive

4. The girl who_____ the next super model is actually a close friend of mine.

   A. ought to be

   B. might be

5. I_____ to a community college at home than go to a big university abroad.

   A. would go

   B. would rather go

Test 2. SENTENCE CORRECTION: Choose the INCORRECT word or phrase and CORRECT it.

1. The room is empty; they left already.

2. Everybody does his duty.

3. We ought water the plants regularly.

4. Jack said that he will have gone to Stanford next year.

5. The movie will have begin by the time we get there.

Lesson 6

ERRORS WITH DANGLING MODIFIERS

ERROR EXAMPLE

WRONG: Having won the world championship for swimming, the Chairman of the Olympic Committee presented the gold medal to the player.

RIGHT: **Having won** the world championship for swimming, the **player** was presented with a gold medal by the Chairman of the Olympic Committee.

GRAMMAR RULES

In English, *-ing* and *-ed* participles are used in phrases which modify the main clause. This structure, also known as DANGLING MODIFIER or DANGLING PARTICIPLE, is usually a *–ing* participial phrase or an *–ed* participial phrase, and this phrase must be followed by a comma and then by the noun or pronoun that is performing the action conveyed by the participle.

Having hidden the new iPhone in her pocket, Mary left the room.

Running across the street, the little dog was hit by a car.

Sitting alone on a big rock on Cypress Mountain, Jennifer was frightened to death by a strange noise.

In the first example, *Mary* performs the action of *having hidden the new iPhone*. In the second example, *the little dog* performs the action of *running across the street*. In the third example, *Jennifer* performs the action of *sitting alone on a big rock on Cypress Mountain.*

To understand more fully the use of the dangling modifiers, check out the following error examples:

>WRONG: Wearing a sparkling red dress, the dog was led out for a walk by the little girl.

>RIGHT: **Wearing** a sparkling red dress, **the little girl** led the dog out for a walk.

>WRONG: Having finished our class, it was time for us to go home.

>RIGHT: **Having finished** our class, **we thought** it was time to go home.

In the first error example, *the little girl* performs the action of *wearing the sparking red dress*. In the second error example, *we* perform the action of *finishing our class*.

PRACTICE TESTS

Test 1. SENTENCE COMPLETION: Choose the CORRECT answer.

1. Having achieved these aims, _____.

   A. he sought to preserve a new European equilibrium through prudence and restraint

   B. a new European equilibrium through prudence and restraint was sought to preserve by him

2. The squirrel, _____ hid its nuts in a variety of places.

   A. tried to prepare for winterr

   B. trying to prepare for winter

3. Wearing a red leather jacket, _____.

   A. the little cat was led out for some fresh air by Mary

   B. Mary led the little cat out for some fresh air

4. Having finished our exam, _____.

   A. it was decided that we go out for a drink

   B. we decided to go out for a drink

5. Running across the street, _____.

   A. a taxi hit Jenny

   B. Jenny was hit by a taxi

Test 2. SENTENCE CORRECTION: Choose the INCORRECT word or phrase and CORRECT it.

1. Having finished dinner, it was time to go to the movies.

2. Being left alone, it was very scary for me in a big house.

3. With its antlers web like the feet of a duck, the North American moose is easy to identify.

4. Anyone interesting in the game can participate.

5. Seeing the business opportunity, a shopping mall was built here by George.

Lesson 7

MISPLACED MODIFIERS: POSITION ADJECTIVES AND ADVERBS CORRECTLY

ERROR EXAMPLE

> WRONG: He began hosting sporadically bug dinner parties, gatherings of friends and friends of friends.
>
> RIGHT: He began **sporadically** hosting bug dinner parties, gatherings of friends and friends of friends.

GRAMMAR RUELS

In English, an adjective normally appears in front of the noun it modifies. For adverbs, it can appear in many positions; however, it cannot come in between a verb and its object.

> The President said that he had something very **urgent** to discuss with me today in the White House.
>
> Michael studies **hard**.
>
> Jack **hardly** studies.

These are the **absolutely essential** words you have to memorize for the TOEFL test.

We have received the most **recent** information about the election.

She said that she had something **very important** to tell us.

WRONG: I have news important to tell you tonight.

RIGHT: I have **important news** to tell you tonight.

WRONG: Jennifer is studying very hard French with the help of a private tutor from Paris.

RIGHT: Jennifer **is studying** French **very hard** with the help of a private tutor from Paris.

PRACTICE TESTS

Test 1. SENTENCE COMPLETION: Choose the CORRECT answer.

1. He _____ when he felt his sickness departing, and became strong and healthy as in the days of his youth.

   A. had tasted scarcely it

   B. had scarcely tasted it

2. To share his expensive apartment downtown, Jacky_____.

   A. is desperately looking for a new roommate

   B. is looking for a new roommate desperately

3. There have been _____ in the new admission agreement.

   A. dramatic changes

   B. changes dramatic

4. Jake mentioned that he had_____to tell us.

   A. highly confidential something

   B. something highly confidential

5. They were very surprised that I_____.

   A. was happy terribly not to accept the prize

   B. was terribly happy not to accept the prize

Test 2. SENTENCE CORRECTION: Choose the INCORRECT word or phrase and CORRECT it.

1. I only have one best friend in New York City.

2. She has bought just a new four-door Ford.

3. We thought it was importantly something we had to do.

4. Michael has been late terrible for class recently.

5. Is there anything with your computer wrong?

Lesson 8

ERRORS WITH PARALLEL STRUCTURE WITH COORDINATE CONJUNCTIONS

ERROR EXAMPLE

WRONG: Jimmy likes to go crab fishing during the day, but Justin prefers catching sharks at night.

RIGHT: Jimmy likes **to go** crab fishing during the day, but Justin prefers **to catch** sharks at night.

GRAMMAR RULES

We use coordinate conjunctions (*and, but, or, yet, for, nor*) to join together equal expressions. These conjunctions can join nouns, verbs, adjectives, phrases, subordinate clauses, and main clauses.

To use them correctly, we must make sure that what is on one side of these coordinate conjunctions must be parallel to what is on the other side. In other words, we must join together two of the same thing.

WRONG: Peter Johnson is not a professor nor is he a lawyer.

RIGHT: Peter Johnson is not a professor **nor** a lawyer.

WRONG: I am not interested in what you are saying about it but your doing it

RIGHT: I am not interested in what you are saying about it **but**

how you are doing it.

WRONG: Jennifer likes hiking and to go fishing.

RIGHT: Jennifer likes hiking **and** fishing.

In the first error example, two nouns *professor* and *lawyer* are joined together by the coordinate conjunction *nor*. In the second error example, two clauses *what you are saying about it* and *how you are doing it* are joined together by the coordinate conjunction *but*. In the third error example, two gerunds *hiking* and *fishing* are joined together by the coordinate conjunction *and*.

The following examples show you how the common types of parallel structures are formed by coordinate conjunctions.

1. TWO VERBS JOINED BY COORDINATE CONJUNCTIONS.

WRONG: David ate and sleeping in the lab when he was writing his research paper.

RIGHT: David ate **and slept** in the lab when he was writing his research paper.

2. TWO ADJECTIVES JOINED BY COORDINATE CONJUNCTIONS.

WRONG: This girl is not truly beautiful and being not smart.

RIGHT: This girl is not truly beautiful **nor** is she smart.

3. TWO PHRASES JOINED BY COORDINATE CONJUNCTIONS.

WRONG: I am not interested in what you are saying about it but your doing it

RIGHT: I am not interested in what you are saying about it **but** how you are doing it.

4. TWO CLAUSES JOINED BY COORDINATE CONJUNCTIONS.

WRONG: She doesn't care about what you do or your survival.

RIGHT: She doesn't care about what you do **or** how you will survive.

PRACTICE TESTS

Test 1. SENTENCE COMPLETION: Choose the CORRECT answer.

1. It is, therefore, imperative that it be shielded from regional and national influence and not_____.

    A. be captured by particular interests

    B. captured by particular interests

2. Nancy suggested taking the plane this evening or _____.

    A. going by train tomorrow

    B. that we go by train tomorrow

3. We are not worried about what you do_____how you are going to take care of your people.

    A. and

    B. but

4. The enemy strapped him, and_____he said nothing.

    A. yet

    B. but

5. A smile costs nothing, _____gives much.

    A. and

    B. but

Test 2. SENTENCE CORRECTION: Choose the INCORRECT word or phrase and CORRECT it.

1. Jennifer thought it was essential that she succeed and skiing regularly.

2. He loved her dearly but not her cat.

3. Jake left his pet rabbit out in the cold and alone.

4. I wanted to go to the party, and Peter never intended to go.

5. Christine worked very hard, and she knew she would not keep her job if she did not.

Lesson 9

ERRORS WITH PARALLEL STRUCTURE WITH CORRELATIVE CONJUNCTIONS

ERROR EXAMPLE

WRONG: Reservation of a necessary portion of an estate shall be made in a will for a successor who neither can work or he has a source of income.

RIGHT: Reservation of a necessary portion of an estate shall be made in a will for a successor who **neither** can work **nor** has a source of income.

GRAMMAR RULES

The paired correlative conjunctions *both... and, either... or, neither... nor,* and *not only... but also, whether...or* are used to join together equal expressions or form parallel structures. And they must join together two of the same thing.

WRONG: He is not only an excellent student but also he is an outstanding athlete.

RIGHT: He is **not only** an excellent student **but also** an outstanding athlete.

WRONG: Mary is neither pretty or charming.

RIGHT: Mary is **neither** pretty **nor** charming

WRONG: The tickets are in my purse or in my pocket.

RIGHT: The tickets are **either** in my purse **or** in my pocket.

The following examples show you how the common types of parallel structures are formed by correlative conjunctions.

1. TWO NOUNS JOINED BY CORRELATIVE CONJUNCTIONS.

Professor MacDonald speaks **neither** French **nor** German.

She is **either** a writer **or** a professor.

2. TWO INFINITIVES JOINED BY CORRELATIVE CONJUNCTIONS.

He wants **either** to go by train **or** to go by plane.

The instructor intends **neither** to please the students **nor** to punish them.

3. TWO ADJECTIVES JOINED BY CORRELATIVE CONJUNCTIONS.

The City of Vancouver is **not only** beautiful **but also** friendly.

This book is **both** well-written **and** professionally designed.

4. TWO PHRASES JOINED BY CORRELATIVE CONJUNCTIONS.

Your luggage is **neither** in the airport **nor** on another plane.

I think I have left my wallet **either** in my car **or** in my office.

5. TWO CLAUSES JOINED BY CORRELATIVE CONJUNCTIONS.

To this day, it's unclear **whether** he shot himself **or** he was murdered.

We know **both** where he will stay **and** what he will do in New York.

PRACTICE TESTS

Test 1. SENTENCE COMPLETION: Choose the CORRECT answer.

1. The children either remained at their estate in Brentwood _____.

A. or left for Los Angeles

   B. and left for Los Angeles

2. The new movie was neither amusing nor_____.

   A. was it interesting.
   B. interesting

3. They are neither interested in our products_____ they willing to do any business with us.

   A. nor are

   B. or are

4. Either he_____ his friends are they people we can trust.

   A. nor

   B. or

5. They have decided not only to help us with the research project_____ to provide support for our finances.

   A. but also

   B. but

Test 2. SENTENCE CORRECTION: Choose the INCORRECT word or phrase and CORRECT it.

1. He is neither well qualified or sufficiently experienced for that position.

2. That horse is not only the youngest one in the race and the only one to win two years in a row.

3. Neither the public or the private sector of the economy will be seriously affected by this regulation.

4. He refused to work either in Chicago nor in Denver.

5. Mary decided not only to start a diet, but to join a fitness club.

Lesson 10

ERRORS WITH PARALLEL STRUCTURE WITH COMPARISONS

ERROR EXAMPLE

> WRONG: The collection of foreign journals in the university library is more extensive than the high school library.
>
> RIGHT: The **collection** of foreign journals in the university library is *more* extensive *than* **that** in the high school library.

GRAMMAR RULES

In making a comparison, we point out the similarities or differences between two things, and those similarities or differences must be in parallel form.

1. We can recognize a comparison showing how two things are different from the *–er… than, more… than* or *less…than.*

   His research for the thesis was *more* useful *than* **hers.**

   Dining in the restaurant is *more* fun *than* **eating** at home.

   This lesson is *more* difficult *than* **that** we had before.

   WRONG: You have fewer homework than they do.

   RIGHT: You have *less* homework *than* they do.

2. We can recognize a comparison showing how two things are the same from the expressions such as *as... as ...*, *the same as...*, *similar to...or like*.

A. *AS...AS...*

    Bill is *as* smart *as* Michael.

    Leone is *as* pretty *as* Jessica.

B. *THE SAME AS...LIKE*

    Mary is *the same* height *as* Bill.

    Tom is *the same* age *as* Peter.

C. *LIKE, THE SAME AS*

    Your car is *like* mine.

    Your car is *the same as* mine.

D. *SIMILAR TO*

    My iPhone is *similar to* yours.

    The economic situation here is very much *similar to* that in Asia.

    WRONG: The IP address is not the same like the IP address of the Windows cluster, but it must be in the same subnet as the Windows cluster.

    RIGHT: The IP address is not **the same as** the IP address of the Windows cluster, but it must be in the same subnet as the Windows cluster.

PRACTICE TESTS

Test 1. SENTENCE COMPLETION: Choose the CORRECT answer.

    1. Our classroom is_____than your seminar room.

        A. much bigger

B. more bigger

2. Vancouver is more beautiful than_____.

   A. any city in North America

   B. any other city in North America

3. We have_____natural resources than any other country in the world.

   A. more

   B. the most

4. Your laptop is just_____mine.

   A. like

   B. the same like

5. Favorable weather is_____than advantageous terrain, and advantageous terrain is less important than unity among the people.

   A. least important

   B. less important

Test 2. SENTENCE CORRECTION: Choose the INCORRECT word or phrase and CORRECT it.

1. Joyce is more smarter than her classmates.

2. This building is more expensive as that one.

3. John's salary was much larger than Tom.

4. The number of college students this year is larger than last year.

5. Susan is more clever than anybody in her class.

Lesson 11

FAULTY SUBJECT-VERB AGREEMENT: SUBJECT WITH APPOSITIVE AND VERB

ERROR EXAMPLE

> WRONG: The Emperor, father of ninety children, were living a very extravagant life.
>
> RIGHT: The **Emperor,** father of ninety children, **was** living a very extravagant life.

GRAMMAR RULES

The subject and the verb in a sentence must agree in person and in number. An appositive is a word or phrase that follows a noun and defines it. It usually has a comma before it and a comma after it.

Remember: never use a verb that agrees with words in the appositive after a subject instead of with the subject itself.

> WRONG: London, the capital of the United Kindom, are not only one of the most beautiful cities in the world but also a university city with the most international students.
>
> RIGHT: **London**, the capital of the United Kindom, **is** not only one of the most beautiful cities in the world but also a university city with the most international students.

WRONG: Cindy Johnson, one of my colleagues, are working for the National Research Institute.

RIGHT: **Cindy Johnson**, one of my colleagues, **is working** for the National Research Institute.

PRACTICE TESTS

Test 1. SENTENCE COMPLETION: Choose the CORRECT answer.

1. Squamish National Park, the free ski resort, _____ the best possible facilities you can ever imagine.

    A. has

    B. have

2. Vancouver Island, the Island of Whales, _____ only two hours away from Vancouver by ferry.

    A. is

    B. are

3. Richard Wilson, famous author of more than eighty books, _____ a reputation of smoking only Cuban cigars.

    A. have

    B. has

4. The beautiful English professor, the queen of romance, _____ recently nominated to receive the Nobel Prize.

    A. was

    B. were

5. Yellow Lake City, the birthplace of the famous poet, _____ now become a major tourist spot in the country.

    A. have

B. has

Test 2. SENTENCE CORRECTION: Choose the INCORRECT word or phrase and CORRECT it.

1. The books, an English dictionary and a chemistry textbook, was on the bookshelf yesterday.

2. Three swimmers from our team, Paul, Edward, and Jim, is in competition for medals.

3. Several pets, two dogs and a cat, needs to be taken care of while we are on vacation.

4. The Empire State University, the largest of state-supported school, have more than 50,000 students on its main campus.

5. This recipe, an old family secret, are an especially important part of our holiday celebrations.

Lesson 12

FAULTY SUBJECT-VERB AGREEMENT: INDEFINITE SUBJECT AND VERB

ERROR EXAMPLE

WRONG: Each of the radioisotopes produced artificially have its own distinct structure.

RIGHT: **Each** of the radioisotopes produced artificially **has** its own distinct structure.

GRAMMAR RULES

In English, when the following pronouns are used as indefinite subjects, they must be followed by singular verbs:

anyone	*either*	*neither*	*what*
anything	*everyone*	*no one*	*whatever*
each	*everything*	*nothing*	*whoever*

1. ANYONE

It's not a job for **anyone** who **is** slow with numbers.

2. EITHER

I will take this route if **either is** acceptable to you.

3. NEITHER

You are not allowed to smoke in this bar **neither is** your partner.

4. WHAT

What goes in will go out. Life is just a cycle.

5. ANYTHING

Anything that **is** expensive is not necessarily good.

6. EVERYONE

Not **everyone thinks** that the government is being particularly generous.

7. NO ONE

No one knows for sure what will happen when the recession

continues.

8. WHATEVER

When you're older I think you're better equipped mentally to cope with **whatever happens**.

9. EACH

Each alternately **claims** it as its own.

10. EVERYTHING

Everything in this room **has** to be kept as it is while I am away.

11. NOTHING

Nothing is impossible in this world if you try hard enough.

12. WHOEVER

Whoever says so, I don't believe it anyway.

The following subjects require either a singular or a plural verb depending on a qualifying phrase or other context from the sentence:

    all   *any*   *some*   *the rest*

1. ALL

    All of the money **has been spent**.

    All of them **have gone** to Whistler for the weekend.

    All is well that **ends** well.

2. ANY

    Clean the mussels and discard **any** that **does not close**.

    Are any of you from the West Coast?

3. SOME

    The terrorized tourists had congregated in the only open bar in town. **Some were** very upset, but others looked as if nothing had happened.

    Their research project is in trouble. **Some** more **money is** needed to keep it going.

4. THE REST

    The **rest needs** no telling.

    The rest of us **are** reprimanded for even the smallest transgression, while he can get away with murder.

PRACTICE TESTS

Test 1. SENTENCE COMPLETION: Choose the CORRECT answer.

    1. I have no doubt, neither_____he, that it was an encounter with God.

        A. do

B. does

2. Any_____ better than none.

   A. are

   B. is

3. Some of this material for some of you_____ very difficult.

   A. is going to be

   B. are going to be

4. Neither of us_____ aware of the fact that it was simply a lie.

   A. were

   B. was

5. Each student_____ required to attend at least half of the total number of assembly meetings each term.

   A. are

   B. is

Test 2. SENTENCE CORRECTION: Choose the INCORRECT word or phrase and CORRECT it.

1. Everyone who has traveled across the United States by car, train, or bus are surprised to see how great the country is.

2. Either of these trains go to Seattle over the weekend.

3. Anyone who wants to win the state lottery have to buy a ticket.

4. The United States and Canada are close neighbors. Neither require that the citizens of the other country have to apply for entry visas.

5. No one who majors in business are allowed to take courses at the School of Music this semester.

Lesson 13

FAULTY SUBJECT-VERB AGREEMENT: COLLECTIVE SUBJECT AND VERB

ERROR EXAMPLE

> WRONG: Because entertaining is such a competitive business, a group of singers or musicians need a manager to help market the music.
>
> RIGHT: Because entertaining is such a competitive business, a **group** of singers or musicians **needs** a manager to help market the music.

GRAMMAR RULES

In English, some collective nouns used as collective subjects may cause problems with the subject and verb agreement. The following is a list of the most common collective subjects (collective nouns) that must agree with singular verbs:

audience	*faculty*	*police*	*variety*
band	*family*	*public*	*2, 3, 4 dollars*
chorus	*group*	*series*	*2, 3, 4 miles*
class	*majority*	*staff*	*committee*
orchestra	*team*		

1. AUDIENCE

The **audience was** quite moved by his passionate speech.

2. FACULTY

The **faculty has agreed on** a change in the requirements.

3. POLICE

The **police has** sufficient evidence to connect the suspect with the explosion.

4. VARIETY

This **variety** of dogs **is** very useful for hunting.

5. BAND

The **band is** just back from a sell-out European tour.

6. FAMILY

The **family has traced** its ancestry to the Norman invaders.

7. PUBLIC

The **public has** to be educated to use resources more effectively.

8. 1,2, 3 DOLLARS

A million dollars is not a big sum for some terribly rich people.

9. CHORUS

The **chorus was** seated above the orchestra.

10. GROUP

The army **group is** shipping out for the Far East today.

11. SERIES

The **series was** based on the autobiography of the author.

12. 2,3,4 MILES

Ten miles is not a short distance for a little girl who has to walk to school everyday.

13. CLASS

The **class starts** in five minutes

Our **class has** twenty-five students from around the world.

14. MAJORITY

The **majority was** determined to press its proposal.

If the **majority decides** to pass the bill, the minorities will benefit the most.

15. STAFF

The **staff** of the school **is** one of the best in the city.

16. COMMITTEE

The **committee was** unable to make a decision whether to fire its president or not.

17. ORCHESTRA

Our **orchestra deserves** ranking with the best in the world.

18. TEAM

Our **team was** left raging at the referee's decision.

To use the above collective subjects correctly, we must remember that never use a plural verb with a collective subject.

NOTE: In certain cases, if we express the separate nature of individuals in a group, a plural verb may be used with the collective subject (collective noun as subject):

The **police are** chasing the murder suspect on the highway now.

PRACTICE TESTS

Test 1. SENTENCE COMPLETION: Choose the CORRECT answer.

1. The chorus_____ very good today. Everybody loved it.

A. was

B. were

2. Such a group of formation_____ briefly referred to as a transformation group.

   A. are

   B. is

3. The committee_____ approved your request to go ahead with the project.

   A. has

   B. have

4. The series_____ one of the most popular and familiar US drama series to Chinese audiences.

   A. are

   B. is

5. Your satisfaction is the greatest support for us and our staff_____ always ready to serve you.

   A. are

   B. is

Test 2. SENTENCE CORRECTION: Choose the INCORRECT word or phrase and CORRECT it.

1. Twenty dollars are the price.

2. The faculty have decided to accept you into our graduate program.

3. The audience usually do not applaud in a church.

4. Four miles are the distance to the office.

5. The staff are meeting in the conference room.

Lesson 14

ERRORS WITH NOUN CLAUSES

ERROR EXAMPLE

    WRONG: He refused to enter a plea could not be determined by the lawyer.

    RIGHT: **Why he refused to enter a plea** could not be determined by the lawyer.

GRAMMAR RULES

A NOUN CLAUSE is a clause that functions as a noun, and it is used in a sentence as either an object of a verb, an object of a preposition, or the subject of the sentence.

    <u>When the contract will be awarded</u> is the question to be answered.

    NOUN CLAUSE AS SUBJECT

    He always talked with <u>whomever he liked</u>.

                     NOUN CLAUSE AS OBJECT

A NOUN CLAUSE, which has its own subject and verb, may be an embedded statement or an embedded question.

1. An embedded statement may be introduced by THAT:

    That the professor has finished grading papers is certain.

2. An embedded question may be introduced by WH-words:

Why **the condition of that patient deteriorated so rapidly** was not explained.

As we know, an English sentence may have more than one clause. The word that connects the clauses is called a CLAUSE CONNECTOR. With regard to NOUN CLAUSES, the most commonly used *NOUN CLAUSES CONNECTORS* are: *what, when, where, why, how, whatever, wherever, whether, if, that.* Be careful to use them correctly with the right patterns.

A. WHAT/WHATEVER

What you have just said is absolutely right.

Whatever you do is none of my business.

B. WHEN

When you want to come to work is up to you.

C. WHY

Nobody knows **why Joyce resigned from such a high-paying job**.

D. HOW

How he got accepted into Princeton University is still a mystery.

E. WHERE/WHEREVER

When you are down, you really don't know **where you can go**.

I will go **wherever I can find my dream job**.

F. WHETHER

Whether they will come to help us is still something unknown.

G. IF

Mary didn't know **if she had done something wrong to drive her boy friend away**.

H. THAT

That he is a good father is known to all in the village.

PRACTICE TESTS

Test 1. SENTENCE COMPLETION: Choose the CORRECT answer.

1. Pug did not know_____was back in her good graces.

   A. he

   B. why he

2. Jack was not sure_____ should take the vacation now.

   A. if he

   B. he

3. He did not_____he had first started to talk aloud when he was by himself.

   A. remember

   B. remember when

4. Sam didn't know _____ have picked up all the right numbers for the Jackpot.

   A. he got to

   B. how he got to

5. I did not know_____my environment that was harming me, or whether I was harming myself.

   A. whether it was

   B. it was

Test 2. SENTENCE CORRECTION: Choose the INCORRECT word or phrase and CORRECT it.

1. Thinking for many centuries that the world was flat.

2. To believe that smoking causes cancer.

3. That Mt. Everest is the highest peak in the world.

4. Do you know what time is the movie to begin?

5. Where do the aliens come from is a mystery.

Lesson 15

USE NOUN CLAUSE CONNECTOR/SUBJECT CORRECTLY

ERROR EXAMPLE

> WRONG: There was a law in the city of Athens which gave to its citizens the power of compelling their daughters to marry whoever they pleased.
>
> RIGHT: There was a law in the city of Athens which gave to its citizens the power of compelling their daughters to marry **whomever** they pleased.

GRAMMAR RULES

We can use NOUN CLAUSE CONNECTORS to introduce noun subject clauses. In some cases a NOUN CLAUSE CONNECTOR is not just a connector; it can also be the SUBJECT of the clause at the same time.

> You can do **whaterver you like** in your spare time as long as you don't get yourself into trouble.
>
> WRONG: We don't know whom will really come to save the poor people in today's society.
>
> RIGHT: We don't know **who will really come to save the poor people in today's society**.

Commonly used NOUN CLAUSE CONNECTOR/SUBJECTS are: *who, what, which, whoever, whatever, whichever*:

1. *Who* and *whoever* **as subject pronouns:**

Whoever comes early can claim the first prize.

WRONG: You can give this used computer to whomever wants it.

RIGHT: You can give this used computer to **whoever** wants it.

2. *What, whatever, which, and whichever* as subject pronouns:

What (whatever) has been stolen in the office is totally up to the police to find out.

Which (whichever) is right is something that you can decide.

WRONG: Whichever interests me most are psychologies, backgrounds, and spotting winners.

RIGHT: **What interests** me most are psychologies, backgrounds, and spotting winners.

PRACTICE TESTS

Test 1. SENTENCE COMPLETION: Choose the CORRECT answer.

1. _____ you say about her is just your personal opinion.

   A. Which

   B. What

2. _____ we should all trust is really hard to say.

   A. Whom

   B. Who

3. _____ is right is up to the judges to decide.

   A. Whom

   B. Which

4. Nobody knows_____ did this horrible thing to her.

A. who

B. whom

5. Stay up to date with the news to see which airports are open and _____ are closed.

   A. what

   B. which

Test 2. SENTENCE CORRECTION: Choose the INCORRECT word or phrase and CORRECT it.

1. I will grab whatever it comes in my way.

2. Whomever has just got out of the window is unknown.

3. The committee will award the prize to whomever is the best.

4. It was hard for us to decide what was the right direction at the crossroads.

5. Dan is whom we believe can help us to design our website.

Lesson 16

USE NOUN CLAUSE CONNECTOR/OBJECT CORRECTLY

ERROR EXAMPLE

WRONG: The employee was unhappy about what it was added to his job description.

RIGHT: The employee was unhappy about **what was added** to his job description.

GRAMMAR RULES

We can use **NOUN CLAUSE CONNECTORS** to introduce noun object clauses. In some cases, a **NOUN CLAUSE CONNECTOR** is not just a connector; it can also be the **OBJECT** of the clause at the same time.

We have to do **whatever it is** necessary to help the poor child.

WRONG: That you choose is totally up to you to decide.

RIGHT: *Whichever* you *choose* is totally up to you to decide.

The following examples show how the **NOUN CLAUSE CONNECTOR/OBJECT** is used. Commonly used **NOUN CLAUSE CONNECTOR/OBJECTS** are: *whom, whomever, what, which, whatever, whichever*:

1. *Whom* and *whomever* as object pronouns:

You can give this book to *whom* you *like*.

WRONG: Whoever you donate this million dollars to is absolutely none of our business.

RIGHT: ***Whomever* you *donate* this million dollars *to*** is absolutely none of our business.

2. *What, whatever, which, and whichever* as object pronouns:

Whatever* we *do should contribute the benefits of the people.

WRONG: The voters should elect whom of the candidates they like best as their district representative.

RIGHT: The voters should elect ***whichever* of the candidates they *like* best as their district representative.**

PRACTICE TESTS

Test 1. SENTENCE COMPLETION: Choose the CORRECT answer.

1. This is a buffet restaurant. You can eat _____ you like.

   A. whatever

   B. which

2. No one knows _____ is the right direction in times of difficulty.

   A. what

   B. which

3. _____ wins the competition will get a million dollars.

   A. Whomever

   B. Whoever

4. We are not sure _____ is responsible for this disaster.

   A. who

B. whom

5. I cannot say with certainty which of my motives are the strongest, but I know_____ of them deserve to be followed.

   A. which

   B. whichever

Test 2. SENTENCE CORRECTION: Choose the INCORRECT word or phrase and CORRECT it.

1. You can give this used computer to who you like.

2. I know about which you did last summer.

3. W are concerned about whom will be elected as our next president.

4. Whoever you love and whatever you do will not affect my life.

5. He was a lucky person and always got whichever he wanted in life.

Lesson 17

ERRORS WITH ADJECTIVE CLAUSES

ERROR EXAMPLE

WRONG: It could have been a simple mistake or misunderstanding, he surely wouldn't have been discharged.

RIGHT: It could have been a simple mistake or misunderstanding, **for which** he surely wouldn't have been discharged.

GRAMMAR RULES

Adjective clauses or relative clauses are a way of joining two sentences together into one sentence. In the joined sentence, the adjective clause modifies a noun or pronoun in the main clause.

The adjective clause is introduced by relative pronouns (*who, whom, whose, that, which*) or relative adverbs (*when, where*). The relative pronouns and relative adverbs that introduce adjective clauses are called CLAUSE MARKERS.

1. **RELATIVE PRONOUNS (*who, whom, whose, that, which*) USED AS CLAUSE MARKERS:**

    The new BMW **which** is selling for more than a hundred thousand dollars is one of the best in the world.

WRONG: Those who live beyond the cell phone, those who have yet to see a computer, those that have no electricity at home are the ones we should care about.

RIGHT: Those who live beyond the cell phone, those who have yet to see a computer, and those **who** have no electricity at home are the ones we should care about.

2. RELATIVE ADVERBS (*when, where*) USED AS CLAUSE MARKERS:

During the time **when** there is hardly any work you can find in America, you might as well try your luck somewhere in Asia.

WRONG: Do not store up for yourselves treasures on earth, which moth and rust destroy, and thieves break in and steal.

RIGHT: Do not store up for yourselves treasures on earth, **where** moth and rust destroy, and thieves break in and steal.

PRACTICE TESTS

Test 1. SENTENCE COMPLETION: Choose the CORRECT answer.

1. 2005 was the year_____I came to the United States.

   A. when

   B. that

2. Paul can still remember_____he first met Lisa.

   A. when

   B. where

3. Hoy is the Professor_____all the students love.

   A. whom

   B. who

4. This is the book_____will change your life forever.

A. who

   B. which

5. The project_____ Jack is responsible is going to be completed by the end of the year.

   A. which

   B. for which

Test 2. SENTENCE CORRECTION: Choose the INCORRECT word or phrase and CORRECT it.

1. He has five brothers who he loves with all his heart.

2. The little mountain village in western Washington is the place that the President was born.

3. The story that he has won the big lottery really unbelievable.

4. We established the charity foundation gave scholarships to qualified students.

5. The way how he got to Harvard Law School virtually known to nobody.

Lesson 18

USE ADJECTIVE CLAUSE MARKERS CORRECTLY

ERROR EXAMPLE

WRONG: I just finished reading the novel whom the professor suggested for my book report.

RIGHT: I just finished reading the novel **which** the professor suggested for my book report.

GRAMMAR RULES

We use an adjective clause to modify a noun. Since the clause functions as an adjective, it is positioned directly after the noun it modifies.

The glass **that** we put on the table contains orange juice.

Connecting words that are used to introduce adjective clauses are called adjective CLAUSE MARKERS. There are two types of clause markers: one is relative pronoun such as *who, whom, whose, which,* or *that*; the other is the relative adverb such as *when* or *where.*

1. LIST OF RELATIVE PRONOUNS USED AS CLAUSE MARKERS:

Who is used as the subject (people) of the adjective clause:

A neurologist is a doctor **who** specializes in the nervous system.

Whom is used as the object (people) of the adjective clause:

This is the man **whom** we just saw at the subway station.

Whose is used as the possessive (people/things) of the noun (usually the subject) of the adjective clause:

This is the computer genius **whose** invention changed our way of life.

Which is used as the subject/object (things) of the adjective clause:

This is the kind of books **which** interest me most.

The melting point is the temperature at **which** a solid changes to a liquid.

That is used as the subject/object (things) of the relative clause:

The famous painting **that** is on display will be auctioned for one million dollars.

The Chinese vase **that** I bought in China last year had had a history of about a thousand years.

2. LIST OF RELATIVE ADVERBS USED AS CLAUSE MAKERS:

Where is used as an adverb of place in the relative clause:

This is the little hut **where** the Nobel Prize winner was born.

When is used as an adverb of time in the relative clause:

Midnight is the usual time **when** famous writers begin to write.

PRACTICE TESTS

Test 1. SENTENCE COMPLETION: Choose the CORRECT answer.

1. He_____ laughs last laughs best.

   A. who

B. whom

2. The girl_____father is an engineer is our college flower.

   A. whose

   B. who's

3. We visited the village_____there were poor people begging for food and clothing.

   A. at which

   B. where

4. The school library_____was built last year is one of the best in the city.

   A. for which

   B. which

5. We will go_____we are needed and whenever we are needed.

   A. wherever

   B. for which

Test 2. SENTENCE CORRECTION: Choose the INCORRECT word or phrase and CORRECT it.

1. Most folk songs are ballads what use simple words and tell simple stories.

2. In addition to being a naturalist, Stewart E. White was a writer his novels describe the struggle for survival on the American frontier.

3. A keystone species is a species of plants or animals its absence has a major effect on an ecological system.

4. The movie which we watched on cable last night it was really frightening.

5. William Samuel Johnson, helped write the Constitution, became the first president of Columbia College in 1787.

Lesson 19

USE ADVERB *TIME* AND *CAUSE* MARKERS CORRECTLY

ERROR EXAMPLE

WRONG: The family suspects a hotel employee, she said, the thieves used a copy of their electronic key to get into their room.

RIGHT: The family suspects a hotel employee, she said, **since** the thieves used a copy of their electronic key to get into their room.

GRAMMAR RULES

An adverb clause consists of a connecting word, called adverb CLAUSE MARKER, and it must have a subject and a verb.

To use the adverb CLAUSE MARKERS correctly, we have to be careful with the following two types of adverb clauses:

1. ADVERB CLAUSE OF TIME

The common adverb *time* markers are: *after, as soon as, once, when, as, before, since, whenever, as long as, by the time, until, while.*

The children had gone to sleep **by the time** I got home last night.

You can't go anywhere **until** you finish your math homework.

We must get everything ready **before** the party begins.

You should come to see me **as soon as** you finish your project.

The plane had already taken off **when** we got to Kennedy Airport.

In the examples above, the adverb clause markers *by the time*, *until*, *before*, *as soon as,* and *when* all introduce *adverb clauses of time*.

2. ADVERB CLAUSE OF CAUSE

The common adverb *cause* markers are: *as, now that, because, since, in as much as, in that.*

In as much as you are well-prepared for the exam, you do not have to be afraid of anything.

David did not get the job **because** he was late for the appointment.

Now that you have got your degree, it is time for you to find a job.

You might as well stay at home **since** there is nothing to do in the office.

Mercury differs from other industrial metals **in that** it is a liquid.

In the examples above, the adverb clause markers *in as much as, because, now that, since,* and *in that* all introduce *adverb clauses of cause*.

PRACTICE TESTS

Test 1. SENTENCE COMPLETION: Choose the CORRECT answer.

1. _____ it is very hard to score high on the test; we must try our best to prepare for the best.

    A. Despite

B. Since

2. We promise that we will not go home_____ we finish our job.

   A. when

   B. until

3. _____ the debtor has no property, I abandoned the claim.

   A. In as much as

   B. when

4. You can call us_____ you need any assistance with your homework or term papers.

   A. whenever

   B. as

5. Sylvia London is an exception_____ she's the only professional psychic in the whole world who has accepted our challenge.

   A. in that

   B. that

Test 2. SENTENCE CORRECTION: Choose the INCORRECT word or phrase and CORRECT it.

1. Tom didn't practice driving, and he failed his road test.

2. They got to the railway station and the train had already left.

3. The graduation party didn't begin as all the students arrived.

4. I have made quite a few friends when I came to New York City.

5. Maple wrote our new business plan while I did the local market research.

Lesson 20

USE ADVERB *CONTRAST*, *CONDITION*, *MANNER*, AND *PLACE* MARKERS CORRECTLY

ERROR EXAMPLE

WRONG: Chanel could run miles in her younger days, now she suffers from joint problems and spends most of her days at home.

RIGHT: **Although** Chanel could run miles in her younger days, now she suffers from joint problems and spends most of her days at home.

GRAMMAR RULES

An adverb clause consists of a connecting word, called adverb CLAUSE MARKER, and it must have a subject and a verb.

To use adverb CLASUE MARKERS correctly, we have to pay special attention to the following types of adverb clauses:

1. **ADVERB CLAUSE OF CONTRAST**

    The common adverb *contrast* markers are: *although, even though, though, while,* and *whereas*

    Even though Mr. Nicolson is not very rich, he is always willing to

    help those in need.

The rich are getting richer and richer **while** the poor are getting poorer and poorer in today's world.

WRONG: We thought she didn't like us; in fact she was very shy.

RIGHT: We thought she didn't like us, **whereas** in fact she was very shy.

2. ADVERB CLAUSE OF CONDITION

The common adverb *condition* markers are: *if, in case, provided, providing, unless,* and *whether.*

If the automobile had not been invented, what would people use for basic transportation?

You will go to Paris with us for the summer **provided** you pass the

State test.

You will never succeed **unless** you try.

WRONG: I will lend you my cell phone but you return it to me in a week.

RIGHT: I will lend you my cell phone **providing** you return it to me in a week.

3. ADVERB CLAUSE OF MANNER

The adverb *manner* markers are: *as, as if,* and *as though.*

When in Rome, do **as** the Romans do.

He looks **as if** he is a multimillionaire.

WRONG: She cried so sadly like the sky was falling down.

RIGHT: She cried so sadly **as though** the sky was falling down.

4. ADVERB CLAUSE OF PLACE

The adverb *place* markers are: *where, wherever.*

When you have nowhere to go, you might as well stay **where** you are.

WRONG: With today's communication tools, you can go to wherever you like to go in a day.

RIGHT: With today's communication tools, you can go **wherever** you like to go in a day.

PRACTICE TESTS

Test 1. SENTENCE COMPLETION: Choose the CORRECT answer.

1. The old woman was moved to tears just_____she had won the lottery.

   A. for

   B. as if

2. Mary is very modest_____she is the best student in our class,

   A. and

   B. although

3. You cannot go to the movie with Jack_____you finish your homework on time.

   A. except for

   B. unless

4. I will not offer any more help to you_____you get straight A's in all your courses next semester.

   A. provided

   B. as

5. Make sure they are all sealed tightly, and keep them in a plastic case or bag_____they leak.

   A. where

   B. in case

Test 2. SENTENCE CORRECTION: Choose the INCORRECT word or phrase and CORRECT it.

1. A good time is where time goes by quickly.

2. I will go with you unless you drive.

3. As you want less noise, you can move to the country.

4. President Kennedy committed the U.S. to being the first to land on the moon, and he died before he saw his dream realized.

5. This secret cove is rumoured to be the place that the first emperor of China was buried.

Lesson 21

USE ADVERB *CAUSE-AND-RESULT MARKERS* CORRECTLY

ERROR EXAMPLE

> WRONG: Albert Einstein was such brilliant a scientist that many of his colleagues had to study for several years in order to form opinions about his theories.

> RIGHT: Albert Einstein was **such a** brilliant scientist that many of his colleagues had to study for several years in order to form opinions about his theories.

GRAMMAR RULES

In an ADVERB CLAUSE OF RESULT introduced by the adverb clause markers *such…that* and *so…that*, the *such/so* clause expresses *CAUSE* and the *that* clause expresses *RESULT*. In each clause, there must be a subject and a verb.

1. ADVERB CLAUSE MARKER: *SUCH…THAT*:

Remember that *such* is used before a count noun or noncount noun followed by *that*. The *such* clause expresses *cause* and the *that* clause expresses *result*.

Water is **such an** excellent solvent **that** it generally contains dissolved materials in greater or lesser amounts.

WRONG: Jenny is such nice girl that everybody loves her.

RIGHT: Jenny is **such a** nice girl **that** everybody loves her.

2. ADVERB CLAUSE MARKER: *SO...THAT*:

Remember that *so* is used before an adjective or an adverb followed by *that*. The *so* clause expresses *cause* and the *that* clause expresses *result*.

The music was **so** loud **that** we could hardly hear anything.

WRONG: By the mid-nineteenth century, land was very expensive in large cities that architects began to conserve space by designing skyscrapers.

RIGHT: By the mid-nineteenth century, land was **so** expensive in large cities **that** architects began to conserve space by designing skyscrapers.

PRACTICE TESTS

Test 1. SENTENCE COMPLETION: Choose the CORRECT answer.

1. Vancouver is _____ nice city that it attracts the most immigrant investors in Canada.

    A. such a

    B. so

2. Jenny is so beautiful _____ all the boys like to go out with her.

    A. so that

    B. that

3. It was _____ early that I could hardly get up.

    A. such an

    B. so

4. Jack is_____ nice young man that everybody in the village loves him.

   A. such
   B. such a

5. The homeless girl drank_____ beer that she could hardly stand up.

   A. much

   B. so much

Test 2. SENTENCE CORRECTION: Choose the INCORRECT word or phrase and CORRECT it.

1. It was so interesting book that he couldn't put it down.

2. She is such nice girl that everyone likes her.

3. We arrived so late as Professor Baker had already called the roll.

4. Preparing frozen foods is too easy that anyone can do it.

5. It is so nice weather that I would like to go out to the beach.

Lesson 22

ERRORS WITH CONDITIONALS: IMPOSSIBLE SITUATION IN PRESENT TIME

ERROR EXAMPLE

    WRONG: If Americans ate fewer foods with sugar and salt, their general health will be better.

    RIGHT: .If Americans **ate** fewer foods with sugar and salt, their general health **would** be better.

GRAMMAR RULES

When we use conditionals which refer to the impossible or unreal situations in present time, we use the Past Tense in the *if*-clause and *would*, *could*, or *might*, + the simple verb in the result clause. The meaning is present, not past.

    WRONG: If we found her luggage, we will call her.

    RIGHT: If we **found** her luggage, we **would call** her.

    WRONG: If drivers obeyed the speed limit, fewer accidents occur.

    RIGHT: If drivers **obeyed** the speed limit, fewer accidents **would occur**.

    WRONG: If I were a bird, I shall fly to New York City for a visit.

RIGHT: If I **were** a bird, I **would fly** to New York City for a visit.

WRONG: If my sister was here, I would not feel so lonely in a foreign country.

RIGHT: If my sister **were** here, I **would not feel** so lonely in a foreign country.

WRONG: If Michael had a million dollars, he will spend it in a week.

RIGHT: If Michael **had** a million dollars, he **would spend** it in a week.

PRACTICE TESTS

Test 1. SENTENCE COMPLETION: Choose the CORRECT answer.

1. If it_____fine, we would go out and play.

   A. was

   B. were

2. If he_____only a few good friends, he would not feel that lonely.

   A. had

   B. has

3. If his parents had enough money, Michael_____have to apply for a student loan.

   A. will not

   B. would not

4. If she_____still young, she would go to Hollywood.

   A. is

B. were

5. If I had the opportunity to meet the president of the company, I_____definitely give my proposal to him in person.

   A. would

   B. will

Test 2. SENTENCE CORRECTION: Choose the INCORRECT word or phrase and CORRECT it.

1. If Jim's family meet Karen, I am sure that they would like her.

2. If you made your bed in the morning, your room looks better when you get back in the afternoon.

3. If Judy didn't drink so much coffee, she wouldn't have been so nervous

4. If you would go to bed earlier, you wouldn't be so sleepy in the morning.

5. If she would eat fewer sweets, she would lose weight.

Lesson 23

ERRORS WITH CONDITIONALS: IMPOSSIBLE SITUATION IN PAST TIME

ERROR EXAMPLE

WRONG: According to some historians, if Napoleon had not invaded Russia, he would conquer the rest of Europe.

RIGHT: According to some historians, if Napoleon **had not invaded** Russia, he **would have conquered** the rest of Europe.

GRAMMAR RULES

When we use conditionals which refer to the impossible or unreal situations in past time, we use the Past Perfect Tense in the *if*-clause and *would*, *could*, or *might* + *have* + the past participle in the result clause. The meaning is past, not present.

WRONG: If I had found her address, I would write her.

RIGHT: If I **had found** her address, I **would have written** her.

WRONG: If she had the opportunity to go to Wall Street, she would have become a billionaire at age twenty-five.

RIGHT: If she **had had** the opportunity to go to Wall Street, she **would have become** a billionaire at age twenty-five.

WRONG: If Marilyn were married to me, she would have become the happiest woman on earth.

RIGHT: If Marilyn **had been married** to me, she **would have become** the happiest woman on earth.

WRONG: If dinosaurs would have continued roaming the earth, man would have evolved quite differently.

RIGHT: If dinosaurs **had continued** roaming the earth, man **would have evolved** quite differently.

PRACTICE TESTS

Test 1. SENTENCE COMPLETION: Choose the CORRECT answer.

1. If he had studied harder, he _____ the exam.

   A. would not have failed

   B. would not fail

2. If she _____ enough money, she would definitely help you.

   A. has

   B. had

3. If I had published my bestseller when I was young, I _____ a millionaire.

   A. would have become

   B. would become

4. If I _____ the scholarship to go to Columbia University, I would have got my Ph.D. in economics.

   A. had

   B. had had

5. If you had treated them fairly, they _____ you without even a notice.

   A. wouldn't have left

   B. wouldn't leave

Test 2. SENTENCE CORRECTION: Choose the INCORRECT word or phrase and CORRECT it.

1. If we had the money, we would have bought a new stereo system.

2. If the neighbors hadn't quieted down, I would have to call the police.

3. If her mother let her, Anne would have stayed longer.

4. If we would have known that she had planned to arrive today, we could have met her at the bus station.

5. If I had more time, I would have checked my paper again.

Lesson 24

ERRORS WITH PASSIVE VOICE

ERROR EXAMPLE

WRONG: If we can't agree by the end of the meeting, the matter will have to take a vote.

RIGHT: If we can't agree by the end of the meeting, a **vote** will **have to be taken** on the matter.

GRAMMAR RULES

Sentences in which the error is an incorrect passive are common in English tests. Therefore, you must be able to determine whether an ACTIVE VOICE or a PASSIVE VOICE of the verb is needed in a sentence.

These cheap shoes **were made** in the Far East. (*Passive Voice*)

We **made** these running shoes for the NBA players. (*Active Voice*)

A new public library **will have to be built** in the city to meet the growing needs of the people.

In recent years, measures **have been taken** to save the forest in the State of Washington.

WRONG: The answer was knew to most of the students before the examination.

RIGHT: The answer **was known** to most of the students before the examination.

WRONG: If you want to be rich, a college education must be received nowadays.

RIGHT: If you want to be rich, **you must receive** a college education nowadays.

WRONG: The whole case of beer was drunk by Michael last night.

RIGHT: **Michael drank** the whole case of beer last night.

WRONG: The authors of this book have been expressed great concern about the environment.

RIGHT: The authors of this book **have expressed** great concern about the environment.

PRACTICE TESTS

Test 1. SENTENCE COMPLETION: Choose the CORRECT answer.

1. Because two team members can commit changes to the same resource, _____.

    A. conflicts can occur and must deal with it.

    B. conflicts can occur and must be dealt with

2. The writer of this article_____great concern about the recession.

A. has been expressed

B. has expressed

3. Great efforts_____ to better the lives of the people in the developing countries.

   A. have made

   B. have been made

4. He_____ that the world is flat.

   A. made to believe

   B. is made to believe

5. This project is too important_____ for our success in this business.

   A. to be neglected

   B. being neglected

Test 2. SENTENCE CORRECTION: Choose the INCORRECT word or phrase and CORRECT it.

1. The whole birthday cake was eaten by John.

2. Bob plays the piano and the guitar is played by him also.

3. The house was bought by my parents in 1980.

4. Most of these toys made in China.

5. Jack made to believe that he was born in a mountain village.

Lesson 25

ERRORS WITH NOUNS

ERROR EXAMPLE

WRONG: Before you bet the bank on your next million dollars idea, you should do a reality check to see if the idea is worth it.

RIGHT: Before you bet the bank on your next **million dollar** idea, you should do a reality check to see if the idea is worth it.

GRAMMAR RULES

One of the most common mistakes at English tests is that a singular noun is used where a plural noun is needed, or a plural noun is used where a singular noun is needed.

Remember that after these key words, *each, every, a, one,* and *single,* a singular noun is used.

We must respect people of all nations; for people from **one nation** may have different customs and habits from another.

Every receipt must be removed from the cashier's drawer and tallied before the store closes everyday.

The rich are getting richer and richer while the poor are getting poorer and poorer with **each** passing **day**.

From now on, I should work hard on my exams **every single day** of the week.

WRONG: With a few exceptions, the benchmark cost of credit in each euro-zone countries is related to the balance of its international debts.

RIGHT: With a few exceptions, the benchmark cost of credit in **each** euro-zone **country** is related to the balance of its international debts.

WRONG: An extended romantic cruise would be a nice way to spend a vacation one days.

RIGHT: An extended romantic cruise would be a nice way to spend a vacation **one day**.

Be careful that after these words, *many, several, both, various,* and *two*, plural nouns should be used.

The automobile repair shop stocked **many parts** for various types of European cars.

We found it hard to believe that **both** of the **pieces** of jewelry had been stolen.

Several students have signed up for the swimming team.

The old professor from Oxford took with him **two mules** loaded with rare books and manuscripts.

WRONG: The auto shop has many parts for various type of expensive European cars.

RIGHT: The auto shop has many parts for **various types** of expensive European cars.

WRONG: On advice from his supervisor, Michael Jones finally got both of his essay published.

RIGHT: On advice from his supervisor, Michael Jones finally got **both** of his **essays** published.

PRACTICE TESTS

Test 1. SENTENCE COMPLETION: Choose the CORRECT answer.

1. A U.S president can only serve a maximum of two_____.

   A. four-years terms

   B. four-year term

2. _____ were very upset after they had learned of the tuition increase next year.

   A. A number of student

   B. A number of students

3. _____ have already agreed to sign the agreement on environment protection.

   A. Several country

   B. Several countries

4. Flowers of_____ caught her eyes as soon as she got into the magic garden of the witch.

   A. various colors

   B. various color

5. Foreign nationals are allowed to stay in the country for up to ninety days with_____.

   A. each entry

   B. each entries

Test 2. SENTENCE CORRECTION: Choose the INCORRECT word or phrase and CORRECT it.

1. Both of my friend are going to Australia to study this fall.

2. Each of the committee member voiced his opinion.

3. Every student should bear his responsibilities to be a good citizen.

4. One of the candidate wants to hold a public debate on campus safety.

5. A number of student activist have voted to establish a poverty fund for college students.

Lesson 26

ERRORS WITH PRONOUNS

ERROR EXAMPLE

WRONG: "Everybody should weigh their words very carefully. What we do not need is alarm in financial markets," she said.

RIGHT: "Everybody should weigh **his** words very carefully. What we do not need is alarm in financial markets," she said.

GRAMMAR RULES

Pronouns are used to replace or refer to nouns, gerunds, infinitives, and sometimes entire clauses. Pronouns change forms depending on their functions in sentences.

Remember that always check personal, possessive, and reflexive pronouns for agreement.

> **They** are the offspring of a great family from Ireland.
>
> Jennifer is a very close friend of **ours**.
>
> Michael likes to brag about **himself** in front of pretty girls.
>
> **We ourselves** are short of supplies because of the storm.
>
> Michael has just got **his** degree in economics from Cambridge University.

The pretty girl doesn't allow anybody to see **her** nor does **she** allow anyone to fall in love with **her**.

WRONG: Everybody.is responsible for cleaning their desk after class.

RIGHT: Everybody is responsible for cleaning **his/her** desk after class.

WRONG: Nobody should be judged by their appearance.

RIGHT: Nobody should be judged by **his** appearance.

WRONG: We must let all citizens know his rights and obligations in the society.

RIGHT: We must let all citizens know **their** rights and obligations in the society.

PRACTICE TESTS

Test 1. SENTENCE COMPLETION: Choose the CORRECT answer.

1. Everyone must sign_____ at the reception desk.

   A. their name

   B. his name

2. He is one of those people who always_____.

   A. brag about themselves

   B. brag about himself

3. Everyone is responsible for _____ own personal safety.

   A. their

   B. his

4. When you live alone off campus, you have to learn how to take care of_____.

   A. yourself

   B. yourselfs

5. They have decided to paint their apartment_____.

   A. theirselves

   B. themselves

Test 2. SENTENCE CORRECTION: Choose the INCORRECT word or phrase and CORRECT it.

1. Between you and I, the economic situation does not look bad.

2. It was him who knocked on the door last night.

3. Jack is as tall as me.

4. You don't have to worry about me. I can cook myself my dinner.

5. It is she, the one whom nobody likes.

Lesson 27

ERRORS WITH REFLEXIVE PRONOUNS

ERROR EXAMPLE

> WRONG: The best ones can take a good idea and use it to transform itself from embryos into giants in a few years, as Amazon and Google have.
>
> RIGHT: The best ones can take a good idea and use it to transform **themselves** from embryos into giants in a few years, as Amazon and Google have.

GRAMMAR RULES

In English, a reflexive pronoun (*myself, ourselves, yourself, yourselves, himself, herself, themselves, itself*) can be used as the complement of a sentence or a clause. It can also be used as the object of a preposition.

> After saving for his whole life, Michael finally built **himself** a huge mansion in the Fraser Valley.
>
> He fixed the car **himself**.
>
> They divided the prize among **themselves**.
>
> WRONG: When you take a test, you should always give you enough time to check the answers before you hand it in.

RIGHT: When you take a test, you should always give **yourself** enough time to check the answers before you hand it in.

WRONG: It seems everyone knows favoritism exists, but nobody wants to put his hand up and say he is guilty of it itself.

RIGHT: It seems everyone knows favoritism exists, but nobody wants to put his hand up and say he is guilty of it **himself**.

PRACTICE TESTS

Test 1. SENTENCE COMPLETION: Choose the CORRECT answer.

1. According to the Fifth Amendment to the U.S. Constitution, nobody should be compelled to be a witness_____.

   A. against themselves

   B. against himself

2. All this would be apart from the failure of two generations of efforts to build a strong European framework_____.

   A. around Germany themselves

   B. around Germany itself

3. She said that she would finish the research project_____.

   A. by herself

   B. for herself

4. Bad memories will not go away_____.

   A. theirselves

   B. of themselves

5. What has happened behind the closed doors is _____.

A. between themselves

   B. themselves

Test 2. SENTENCE CORRECTION: Choose the INCORRECT word or phrase and CORRECT it.

   1. Be careful with these sharp tools or you will hurt to you.

   2. A child cannot feed self by the age of five months.

   3. Since nobody knew how to swim in my family, I had to teach me how

      to swim.

   4. Help you to whatever you like, it is free.

   5. A modern microwave that can clean it is really unbelievable.

Lesson 28

ERRORS WITH PRONOUN REFERENCES

ERROR EXAMPLE

WRONG: And when it comes to fathering healthy children, older men, it turns out, are just as much at the mercy of its biological clocks as women.

RIGHT: And when it comes to fathering healthy children, older **men**, it turns out, are just as much at the mercy of **their** biological clocks as women.

GRAMMAR RULES

A pronoun must clearly refer to the noun or noun phrase for which it substitutes. Remember that every pronoun or possessive agrees with the noun or noun phrase it refers to in number and in person.

Since you can clean the room **yourself**, why do you have to pay to hire somebody else to do it?

Everyone should always bear in mind that he is always responsible for **himself** and the society.

WRONG: When children experience too much frustration, its behavior ceases to be integrated.

RIGHT: When **children** experience too much frustration, **their** behavior ceases to be integrated.

WRONG: Mary paid more attention to her dog than its baby girl.

RIGHT: **Mary** paid more attention to her dog than **her** baby girl.

WRONG: The committee and their members all voted in his favor.

RIGHT: The **committee** and **its** members all voted in his favor.

PRACTICE TESTS

Test 1. SENTENCE COMPLETION: Choose the CORRECT answer.

1. It seems we all know that discrimination exists, but we do not want to put _____.

   A. our hands up and say we are guilty of it ourselves

   B. his hand up and say he is guilty of it himself

2. Although the destruction that _____ is often terrible, cyclones benefit a much wider belt than they devastate.

   A. they cause

   B. it causes

3. Those who come early can help_____with some coffee and donuts.

   A. itself

   B. themselves

4. Nobody is allowed to leave this room without finishing_____exam.

   A. his

   B. their

5. If the students decide to take the reading break next week, they have to get the permission_____supervisors.

   A. from its

   B. from their

Test 2. SENTENCE CORRECTION: Choose the INCORRECT word or phrase and CORRECT it.

1. Nobody should be judged by their appearance.
2. We must let all citizens know his rights and obligations in the society.
3. He is one of those people who always brag about himself.
4. The current world situation gives the people in rich countries more opportunities than the friends in poor countries.
5. The students are trying their best to help the classmates in need.

Lesson 29

ERRORS WITH ADJECTIVES AND ADVERBS

ERROR EXAMPLE

> WRONG: Due to the island's healing powers the baby will grow abnormal faster and be born in a few weeks.
>
> RIGHT: Due to the island's healing powers the baby will grow **abnormally** faster and be born in a few weeks.

GRAMMAR RULES

In English, adjectives and adverbs have different functions in a sentence. Basically, an adjective is used to modify a noun or a pronoun.

> She is **pretty smart** in real estate investment.
>
> This **beautiful** poem is **absolutely** the best I have ever read.
>
> Her **friendly** gestures moved me almost to tears.
>
> WRONG: Modern art is on display at the Guggenheim Museum, a building with an unusually design.
>
> RIGHT: Modern art is on display at the Guggenheim Museum, a

building with an **unusual** design.

An adverb is used to modify a verb, an adjective or another adverb.

This is an **extremely important** matter that needs to be attended to **immediately**.

The wild nature of this man shocked everybody in the room when he picked a fork and stabbed the toy cat **uncannily**.

The dramatic turn in life sometimes triggers one's desire to do something **absolutely** beyond one's control.

WRONG: Our offshore telephone call centers were successful established in 2005.

RIGHT: Our offshore telephone call centers were **successfully** established in 2005.

WRONG: I worked real hard on Microeconomics, but failed.

RIGHT: I worked **really hard** on Microeconomics, but failed.

PRACTICE TESTS

Test 1. SENTENCE COMPLETION: Choose the CORRECT answer.

1. The newly released Hollywood movie tells an_____ moving story.

   A. extreme

B. extremely

2. Mary Lopez got almost full marks on her biology final because she _____ for it.

   A. had studied very hardly

   B. had studied very hard

3. The _____ scared even the bravest man in the world.

   A. rare disease

   B. rarely disease

4. _____ had Thomas Boss got home, it began to rain.

   A. Hard

   B. Hardly

5. The handsome young man spoke _____ that everybody thought he was a professor from Oxford.

   A. so profoundly

   B. so profound

Test 2. SENTENCE CORRECTION: Choose the INCORRECT word or phrase and CORRECT it.

1. Jake was extreme happy to see her coming back from vacation in Africa.

2. The deadly silence of the night even scared the bravest soldiers.

3. You must do it very carefully, if not perfect.

4. He worked very hardly on his college entrance exams.

5. You should order that book real soon.

Lesson 30

ERRORS WITH COMPARATIVES AND SUPERLATIVES

ERROR EXAMPLE

WRONG: Perhaps more than any place in Asia, Hong Kong's energy comes from a powerful relationship with the present.

RIGHT: Perhaps more than **any other** place in Asia, Hong Kong's energy comes from a powerful relationship with the present.

GRAMMAR RULES

There are three kinds of comparison in English. They are the equative, comparative, and the superlative.

1. Equative degree is used to show equality.

This building is **as** tall **as** that one.

This building is **the same** height **as** that one.

WRONG: This building is as tall like that one by the seaside.

RIGHT: This building is **as** tall **as** that one by the seaside.

WRONG: Although we often use "speed" and "velocity" interchangeably, in a technical sense, "speed" is not always as "velocity".

RIGHT: Although we often use "speed" and "velocity" interchangeably, in a technical sense, "speed" is not always **the same as** "velocity."

2. The comparative degree is used to compare two things that are not equal. In your test, when you see the word *more*, look for *than*.

To use comparatives correctly, pay special attention to the following rules:

A. One syllable or two syllable adjectives ending in *–y,* change the *–y* to *–i* before adding *–er.*

Susan is busy, but her mother is even **busier**.

She is pretty, but her sister is **prettier**.

WRONG: If you are happy here, I am even more happier.

RIGHT: If you are happy here, I am even **happier**.

B. We put *more* before the adjective if it has two or three syllables to form the comparative.

Tom is handsome, but his brother is **more handsome**.

Life in the country is enjoyable, but life in the city is **more enjoyable.**

WRONG: She looks gorgeous, but her younger sister looks the most gorgeous.

RIGHT: She looks gorgeous, but her younger sister looks **more gorgeous.**

C. Remember that *than* is the only structure word that can follow comparatives.

This tree is definitely **taller than** that one.

Jennifer is **more trustworthy than** her elder sister.

WRONG: Michael is definitely more smarter than Jack Daniels.

RIGHT: Michael is definitely **smarter** than Jack Daniels.

3. **The superlative degree is used to compare three or more things that are not equal. When you see the words like *one of the*, look for *most* or a word ending in *–est*.**

To use superlatives correctly, pay special attention to the following rules:

A. One syllable or two syllable adjectives ending in *–y,* change the *–y* to *–i* before adding *–est* .

Jenny is prettier than Michelle, but Helen is the **prettiest** of the three.

B. We put *the most* before the adjective if it has two or three syllables to form the superlative.

Joyce is more charming than Lucy, but Shiny is the **most charming**.

Vancouver is one of the **most beautiful** cities in the world.

WRONG: One of the most exciting thing for parents is a baby's first word spoken like a miracle.

RIGHT: **One of** the most exciting **things** for parents is a baby's first word spoken like a miracle.

PRACTICE TESTS

Test 1. SENTENCE COMPLETION: Choose the CORRECT answer.

1. Vancouver is more beautiful_____ in the world.

   A. than any city

   B. than any other city

2. He is the _____ person in the class to be late.

A. least possible

   B. less possible

3. Jenny Jackson, our college flower, is _____ girl on campus.

   A. more beautiful than any

   B. more beautiful than any other

4. Between the twin brothers, Thomas is _____.

   A. the tallest

   B. the taller of the two

5. Seattle is _____ in the United States.

   A. the most livable city

   B. more livable than any other cities

Test 2. SENTENCE CORRECTION: Choose the INCORRECT word or phrase and CORRECT it.

1. Our building is the same height like yours.

2. Jennifer is definitely smart as Marilyn.

3. The population of my hometown is much smaller than Shanghai.

4. The higher the degree you have, the more high wage you will get.

5. One of the most difficult problem in math is logical reasoning.

Lesson 31

ERRORS WITH ARTICLES

ERROR EXAMPLE

> WRONG: That's such a deep question. Yeah. Is a virtual world likely to be an Utopia, would be one way I'd say it.
>
> RIGHT: That's such a deep question. Yeah. Is a virtual world likely to be **a** Utopia, would be one way I'd say it.

GRAMMAR RULES

In English, there are two kinds of articles: indefinite articles *a* and *an* and definite article *the*.

For indefinite Articles, the basic difference between *a* and *an* is that *a* is used in front of consonants and *an* is used in front of vowels {*a, e, i, o, u*).

> Mary just bought **a** copy of the new Riverside Shakespeare.
>
> The old man talked with me for about **an** hour and half.
>
> Life is **an** infinite journey to the unknown.
>
> WRONG: It is an universal fact that we have only one earth.
>
> RIGHT: It is **a** universal fact that we have only one earth.

The definite article *the* is used with singular and plural nouns or the nouns referring to things we already know about.

> Seattle is one of the most beautiful cities in the United States.

A stranger attempted to abduct **the** little girl near **the** school.

The professor from MIT spoke about his new design yesterday.

WRONG: Michael is a player you can count on for success.

RIGHT: Michael is **the** player you can count on for success.

PRACTICE TESTS

Test 1. SENTENCE COMPLETION: Choose the CORRECT answer.

1. The scholarship that Philip received to study finance at Harvard University presented_____.

    A. a unique opportunity

    B. an unique opportunity

2. _____ responds to a wide range of frequencies.

    A. An human ear

    B. A human ear

3. Vancouver is _____ of dreams for new immigrants.

    A. the city

    B. a city

4. The farm workers have to work more than ten hours a day except for_____hour for lunch break during the summer.

    A. a

    B. an

5. The earth travels at_____high rate of speed around_____sun.

    A. the....the

B. a...the

Test 2. SENTENCE CORRECTION: Choose the INCORRECT word or phrase and CORRECT it.

1. We went to the store and bought new stove.

2. It is always difficult to make the decisions.

3. She doesn't have understanding of the subject yet.

4. Dogs make the good pets.

5. The honesty is a virtue.

Lesson 32

ERRORS WITH PREPOSITIONS

ERROR EXAMPLE

WRONG: Israel's Prime Minister Ehud Olmert said Israeli forces will abstain of attacking the Gaza Strip if militants stop firing rockets.

RIGHT: Israel's Prime Minister Ehud Olmert said Israeli forces will **abstain from** attacking the Gaza Strip if militants stop firing rockets.

GRAMMAR RULES

We use prepositions to show the relationships between their objects and other words in the sentence.

After waiting **for** an hour and half, the bus finally **arrived at** Lougheed Town Centre Station.

All men are equal. We should never **look down upon** anybody.

The following are the most common kinds of relationships that the prepositions can show:

1. Place (*in, on, under, over*, etc.)

I parked my car **under** a big tree.

There is a world map **on** the wall.

WRONG: There is a new bridge on the river.

RIGHT:　　There is a new bridge **over** the river.

2. Direction (*to, toward, into,* etc.)

The children rushed **into** the room.

He is going **toward** the garden.

WRONG: Go straight for the top of the mountain and then you can see the whole city.

RIGHT:　　Go straight **to** the top of the mountain and then you can see the whole city.

3. Time (*in, on, at,* etc.)

Those who want to go to the show will meet **at** two o'clock.

We will go to New York **on** Friday.

WRONG: We got to the station in around five.

RIGHT:　　We got to the station **at** around five.

4. Agent (*by*)

These toys were handmade **by** her mother.

This novel was written **by** a school girl.

WRONG: The young artist earns her living of painting pictures for tourists in the park.

RIGHT:　　The young artist earns her living **by** painting pictures for tourists in the park.

5. Instrument (*by, with*)

We went to Whistler **by** train.

He opened the box **with** a strange key.

WRONG: She heard the news from telephone.

RIGHT: She heard the news **by** telephone.

6. Accompaniment (*with*)

I like coffee **with** cream and sugar.

He went to the library **with** his girl friend.

WRONG: We will always stay around you no matter what happens.

RIGHT: We will always stay **with** you no matter what happens.

7. Purpose (*for*)

She went to Safeway **for** some groceries.

Tom went to his teacher **for** some help.

WRONG: These animals migrated south of food and better climate.

RIGHT: These animals moved south **for** food and better climate.

8. Measure (b*y, of*)

We buy beef **by** the pound.

Could I have a quart **of** milk?

WRONG: This farmer sells his corns of sacks.

RIGHT: This farmer sells his corns **by** sacks.

PRACTICE TESTS

Test 1. SENTENCE COMPLETION: Choose the CORRECT answer.

1. Every summer I would go to live_____ for a month.

    A. on my grandpa's snake farm

    B. at my grandpa's snake farm

2. The two little girls divided the big cake_____.

    A. between themselves

    B. among themselves

3. I am sorry I can't go with you tonight because I have a lot of things to_____.

    A. take care

    B. take care of

4. We do look forward_____ you in New York if you decide to come back for the holidays.

    A. to see

    B. to seeing

5. Since everybody is born equal, we should never_____ those who are poor and unfortunate.

    A. look down

    B. look down upon

Test 2. SENTENCE CORRECTION: Choose the INCORRECT word or phrase and CORRECT it.

1. My grandpa lives in a snake farm in Arizona.

2. This store sells flour for the pound.

3. Do you think that Jack walks as his fat.

4. These artifacts were made from the Indians.

5. There is a big hole on the wall.

ANSWER KEY

Lesson 1

Test 1:

1. B

2. B (Here simple past tense should be used: *became;* for it refers to the action that began and ended in the past.)

3. A

4. A

5. B

Test 2:

1. By the time I got to the airport, the plane **had** already **taken off**.

2. I **have traveled** to five major cities since I cam to the United States last year.

3. The ground is wet. It must **have rained**.

4. I **was taking** a shower when Helen called me last night.

5. By the end of 2005, I **had** already **finished** my bachelor's degree in computer science at the University of Rochester.

Lesson 2

Test 1:

1. B

2. B (Here present perfect tense should be used: *have heard*; for the action still relates to the present.)

3. A

4. B

5. B

Test 2:

1. After I **have completed** my studies in America, I will return to my own country.

2. When Jennifer began her schooling, she **had** already **memorized** more than 500 new words.

3. Since I **have grown** up now, I should help my parents in finances.

4. Up to now, the city **has built** five community centres.

5. By the end of 1988, the number of international students in the country **had risen** to two million.

Lesson 3

Test 1:

1. A
2. B
3. A
4. B
5. A

Test 2:

1. **Have** you **talked** to the Department Chair *jet?*

2. Jenny **has** never **had** lobsters *before.*

3. He **has waited** for you *for a long time.*

4. *Since 1979* great changes **have taken** place in my hometown.

5. *By 2006* our city **had built** more than thirty public libraries.

Lesson 4

Test 1:

1. B (Here **exhausted** should be

    used because it is a past participle used as an adjective and it has a passive meaning.)

2. B (Here after *afford*, an infinitive **to heat** must be used instead of a gerund.)

3. B
4. B
5. A

Test 2:

1. This new sports car is very easy **to drive.**

2. The most important discovery **known** to all might be DNA.

3. No rich person can afford *to* **feed** such a hungry nation after the war.

4. **Having finished** dinner, we took a walk along the Thames.

5. No one looks forward to **hearing** bad news after the college entrance exam.

2. Everybody **should** do his duty.

3. We **must** water the plants regularly.

4. Jack said that he **might go** to Stanford next year.

5. The movie **will have begun** by the time we get there.

Lesson 5

Test 1:

1. B
2. B
3. A
4. B
5. B

Test 2:

1. The room is empty; they **must have left** already.

Lesson 6

Test 1:

1. A (**Having achieved... he sought to preserve**: here *he* is the performer of both actions in the dangling participle and the main sentence)

2. B (**trying to prepare...hid**, the performer of both actions is the squirrel)

3. B
4. B
5. B

- 123 -

Test 2:

1. Having finished dinner, **we thought** it was time to go to the movies.

2. Being left alone, **I felt** it was very scary in a big house.

3. With its antlers **webbed like** the feet of a duck, the North American moose is easy to identify.

4. Anyone **interested** in the game can participate.

5. Seeing the business opportunity, **George** built a shopping mall here.

Lesson 7

Test 1:

1. B (had **scarcely** tasted it: never place an adverb in between a verb and its object.)

2. A (is **desperately** looking)

3. A

4. B

5. B

Test 2:

1. I have **only** one best friend in New York City.

2. She has **just** bought a new four-door Ford.

3. We thought it was something **important** we had to do.

4. Michael has been **terribly** late for class recently.

5. Is there anything **wrong** with your computer?

Lesson 8

Test 1:

1. A (**it be captured**: use the same kind of passive voice like *it be shielded*)

2. A (**taking going**…are of the same thing: *gerunds*.)

3. B

4. A

5. B

Test 2:

1. Jennifer thought it was essential that **she succeed** *and* **that she ski** regularly.

2. He **loved her** dearly *but* he **did not love her cat**.

3. Jake left his pet rabbit **out in the cold** *and* **by itself**.

4. I wanted to go to the party, **yet** Peter never intended to go.

5. Christine worked very hard; **for** she knew she would not keep her job if she did not.

Test 2:

1. He is **neither** well qualified **nor** sufficiently experienced for that position.

2. That horse is **not only** the youngest one in the race **but also** the only one to win two years in a row.

3. **Neither** the public **nor** the private sector of the economy will be seriously affected by this regulation.

4. He refused to work **either** in Chicago **or** in Denver.

5. Mary decided **not only** to start a diet, **but also** to join a fitness club.

Lesson 9

Lesson 10

Test 1:

1. A (**either   or**)

2. B (**neither amusing...**

   nor interesting...are of

   the same thing: *adjectives*)

3. A

4. B

5. A

Test 1:

1. A

2. B

3. A

4. A

5. B

Test 2:

1. Joyce is **smarter** *than* her classmates.

2. This building is ***more*** expensive *than* that one.

3. John's salary was much larger *than* **Tom's**

4. The number of college students this year is larger *than* **that of** last year.

5. Susan is ***more*** clever ***than* any other student** in her class.

Lesson 11

Test 1:

1. A
2. A
3. B
4. A
5. B

Test 2:

1. **The books**, an English dictionary and a chemistry textbook, **were** on the bookshelf yesterday.

2. **Three swimmers** from our team, Paul, Edward, and Jim, **are** in competition for medals.

3. **Several pets**, two dogs and a cat, **need** to be taken care of while we are on vacation.

4. **The Empire State University**, the largest of state-supported school, **has** more than 50,000 students on its main campus.

5. **This recipe**, an old family secret, **is** an especially important part of our holiday celebrations.

Lesson 12

Test 1:

1. B
2. B
3. A
4. B
5. B

Test 2:

1. **Everyone** who has traveled across the United States by car, train, or bus **is** surprised

to see how great the country is.

2. **Either** of these trains **goes** to Seattle over the weekend.

3. **Anyone** who wants to win the state lottery **has** to buy a ticket.

4. The United States and Canada are close neighbors. **Neither requires** that the citizens of the other country have to apply for entry visas.

5. **No one** who majors in business **is** allowed to take courses at the School of Music this semester.

Lesson 13

Test 1:

1. A
2. B
3. A
4. B
5. B

Test 2:

1. **Twenty dollars** *is* the price.

2. The **faculty has decided** to accept you into our graduate program.

3. The **audience** usually *does not applaud* in a church.

4. **Four miles** *is* the distance to the office.

5. The **staff** *is* meeting in the conference room.

Lesson 14

Test 1:

1. B
2. A
3. B
4. B
5. A

Test 2:

1. It was thought for many centuries **that the world was flat**.

2. It is believed **that smoking causes cancer**.

3. **That Mt. Everest is the highest peak in the world** is known to all.

4. Do you know **what time the movie is to begin**?

5. **Where the aliens come from** is a mystery.

Lesson 15

Test 1:

1. B
2. A
3. B
4. A
5. B

Test 2:

1. I will grab **whatever comes in my way.**

2. **Whoever has just got out of the window** is unknown.

3. The committee will award the prize to **whoever is the best.**

4. It was hard for us to decide **which was the right direction at the crossroads.**

5. Dan is **who** we believe **can help us to design our website.**

Lesson 16

Test 1:

1. A
2. B
3. B
4. A
5. A

Test 2:

1. You can give this used computer to *whomever* you *like.*

2. I know *what* you *did* last summer.

3. We are concerned about *who will be elected* as our next president.

4. *Whomever* you *love* and whatever you do will not affect my life.

5. He was a lucky person and always got *whatever* he *wanted* in life.

Lesson 17

Test 1:

1. A
2. B
3. A
4. B
5. B

Test 2:

1. He has five brothers **whom** he loves with all his heart.

2. The little mountain village in western Washington is the place **where** the President was born.

3. The story **that** he has won the big lottery is really unbelievable.

4. We established the charity foundation **which** gave scholarships to qualified students.

5. The way by **which** he got to Harvard Law School is virtually known to nobody.

Lesson 18

Test 1:

1. A

2. A
3. B
4. B
5. A

Test 2:

1. Most folk songs are ballads **which** use simple words and tell simple stories

2. In addition to being a naturalist, Stewart E. White was a writer **whose** novels describe the struggle for survival on the American frontier.

3. A keystone species is a species of plants or animals **whose** absence has a major effect on an ecological system.

4. The movie **that** we watched on cable last night **was** really frightening.

5. William Samuel Johnson, **who** helped write the Constitution, became the first president of Columbia College in 1787.

Lesson 19

Test 1:

1. B
2. B
3. A
4. A
5. A

Test 2:

1. **Because** Tom didn't practice driving, he failed his road test.
2. **By the time** they got to the railway station, the train had already left.
3. The graduation party did not begin **until** all the students arrived.
4. I have made quite a few friends **since** I came to New York City.
5. Maple wrote our new business plan, **and** I did the local market research.

Lesson 20

Test 1:

1. B
2. B
3. B
4. A
5. B

Test 2:

1. A good time is **when** time goes by quickly.
2. I will go with you **provided that** you drive.
3. **If** you want less noise, you can move to the country.
4. President Kennedy committed the U.S. to being the first to land on the moon, **but** he died before he saw his dream realized.
5. This secret cove is rumoured to be the place **where** the first emperor of China was buried.

Lesson 21

Test 1:

1. A
2. B
3. B

4. B

5. B

Test 2:

1. It was **such an** interesting book **that** he couldn't put it down.

   (or It was **so** interesting **a** book **that** he couldn't put it down.)

2. She is **such a** nice girl **that** everyone likes her.

   (or She is **so** nice **a** girl **that** everyone likes her.)

3. We arrived **so** late **that** Professor Baker had already called the roll.

4. Preparing frozen foods is **so** easy **that** anyone can do it.

5. It is **such** nice weather **that** I would like to go out to the beach.

Lesson 22

Test 1:

1. B
2. A

3. B
4. B
5. A

Test 2:

1. *If* **Jim's family met** Karen, I am sure that **they would like** her.

   or

   I am sure that **they would like** her *if* **Jim's family met** Karen.

2. *If* **you made** your bed in the morning, **your room would look** better when you get back in the afternoon.

   or

   Your room would look better when you get back in the afternoon *if* **you made** your bed in the morning.

3. *If* **Judy didn't drink** so much coffee, **she wouldn't be** so nervous.

   Or

   Judy wouldn't be so nervous *if* **she didn't drink** so much coffee.

4. ***If* you went** to bed earlier, **you wouldn't be** so sleepy in the morning.

or

You wouldn't be so sleepy in the morning **if you went** to bed earlier.

5. ***If* she ate** fewer sweets, **she would lose** weight.

or

She would lose weight **if she ate** fewer sweets.

Lesson 23

Test 1:

1. A
2. B
3. A
4. B
5. A

Test 2:

1. ***If* we had had** the money, **we would have bought** a new stereo system.

or

We would have bought a new stereo system *if* **we had had** the money.

2. ***If* the neighbors hadn't quieted down, I would have had** to call the police.

or

I would have had to call the police *if* **the neighbors hadn't quieted down**.

3. ***If* her mother had let** her, **Anne would have stayed** longer.

or

Anne would have stayed longer *if* **her mother had let** her.

4. ***If* we had known** that she had planned to arrive today, **we could have met** her at the bus station.

or

We could have met her at the bus station *if* **we had known** that she had planned to arrive today.

5. *If* **I had had** more time, **I would have checked** my paper again.

or

I would have checked my paper again *if* **I had had** more time.

Lesson 24

Test 1:

1. B (**conflicts must be dealt with**)

2. B (**has expressed**, the active voice is needed here)

3. B

4. B

5. A

Test 2:

1. John **ate** the whole birthday cake.

2. Bob **plays the piano** and also **the guitar**.

3. My **parents bought** the house in 1980.

4. Most to these toys **were made** in China.

5. Jack **was made** to believe that he was born in a mountain village.

Lesson 25

Test 1:

1. B (Here it should be **four-year** instead of *four-years* because when a noun is used as an adjective, it should be in the singular form.)

2. B (After *a number of*, always use plural noun.)

3. B

4. A

5. A

Test 2:

1. Both of my **friends** are going to Australia to study this fall.

2. Each of the committee **members** voiced his opinion.

3. Every student should bear his **responsibility** to be a good citizen.

4. One of the **candidates** wants to hold a public debate on campus safety.

5. A number of student **activists** have voted to establish a poverty fund for college students. (Here *student* is a noun used as an adjective modifying activists; therefore, it should be singular.)

Lesson 26

Test 1:

1. B (Here **everyone** is the third person singular, therefore, the possessive pronoun should be *his*.)

2. A (Here you should use reflexive pronoun **themselves** because it refers to *people*.)

3. B

4. A

5. B

Test 2:

1. Between you and **me**, the economic situation does not look bad.

2. It was **he** who knocked on the door last night.

3. Jack is as tall as **I**.

4. You don't have to worry about me. I can cook dinner **myself**.

5. It is **her**, the one whom nobody likes.

Lesson 27

Test 1:

1. B (Here **nobody** is the third person singular, therefore, *himself* should be used.)

2. B (Here **Germany** is the third person singular, therefore, *itself* should be used.)

3. A

4. B

5. A

Test 2:

1. Be careful with these sharp tools or you will hurt **yourself**.

2. A child cannot feed **himself** by the age of five months.

3. Since nobody knew how to swim in my family, I had to teach **myself** how to swim.

4. Help **yourself** to whatever you like, it is free.

5. A modern microwave that can clean **itself** is really unbelievable.

Lesson 28

Test 1:

1. A (**we   our**)

2. A (**they   cyclones**)

3. B

4. A

5. B

Test 2:

1. **Nobody** should be judged by **his** appearance.

2. We must let all **citizens** know **their** rights and obligations in the society.

3. He is one of those **people** who always brag about **themselves**.

4. The current world situation gives the **people** in rich countries more opportunities than **their** friends in poor countries.

5. The **students** are trying their best to help **their** classmates in need.

Lesson 29

Test 1:

1. B (Here we must use **extremely** instead of *extreme* because extremely is an adverb of degree and it

is here used to modify the adjective *moving*.)

2. B (Here **hard** must be used because *hardly* means *almost not*)

3. A

4. B

5. A

Test 2:

1. Jake was **extremely** happy to see

   her coming back from

   vacation in Africa.

2. The **dead** silence of the night

   even scared the bravest

   soldiers.

3. You must do it very

   carefully, if not **perfectly**.

4. He worked very **hard** on his

   college entrance exams.

5. You should order that book

   really soon.

Lesson 30

Test 1:

1. B (Here you should

   use **than any other** *city*

   instead of *than any*

   city because any city

   includes Vancouver itself.)

2. A (Here you should use **least** because there must be at least three or more students in a class.)

3. B

4. B

5. A

Test 2:

1. Our building is **the same** height **as** yours.

2. Jennifer is definitely **as** smart **as** Marilyn.

3. The population of my hometown is much smaller than **that of** Shanghai.

4. The higher the degree you have, the **higher** the wage you will get.

5. One of the most difficult **problems** in math is logical reasoning.

Lesson 31

Test 1:

1. A (use **an** only with words beginning with a vowel sound)

2. B (use ***an*** only with words beginning with a vowel sound)

3. B

4. B

5. B

Test 2:

1. We went to the store and bought **a** new stove.

2. It is always difficult to **make decisions**.

3. She doesn't have **an** understanding of the subject yet.

4. Dogs make **good pets**.

5. **Honesty** is a virtue.

Lesson 32

Test 1:

1. A

2. A

3. B

4. B

5. B

Test 2:

1. My grandpa lives **on** a snake farm in Arizona.

2. This store sells flour **by** the pound.

3. Do you think that Jack walks **like** his father?

4. These artifacts were made **by** the Indians.

5. There is a big hole **in** the wall.

INDEX

The numbers in the index are lesson numbers, not page numbers.

A

a 25, 31
active meaning 4
active voice 24
adjective 29
adjective clause 17
adjective clause marker 18
admit 4
adverb 29
adverb *cause-and-result* marker 21
adverb clause of cause 19
adverb clause of condition 20
adverb clause of contrast 20
adverb clause of manner 20
adverb clause of place 20
adverb clause of time 19
agree 4
all 12
already 1, 3
and 8
any 12
anyone 12
anything 12
appreciate 4
article 31
as...as 10
at 32
audience 13

avoid **4**

B

band **13**
base form of the verb 5
be accustomed to **4**
be interested in **4**
be opposed to **4**
be used to **4**
both 25
both...and **9**
but 8
by **32**
by + time **3**

C

can 5
cannot help **4**
care **4**
chorus **13**

class **13**
collective subject 13
committee **13**
comparative 30
comparative degree 30, 10
conditionals (subjunctive mood) 22, 23
consider **4**
could 5

D

dangling modifier 6
dangling participle 6
decide **4**
decide on **4**
definite article 31
deny **4**
deserve **4**
direct speech 5
during **1**

E

each 25, 12

either 12

either...or 9

enjoy 4

equative degree 30

every 25

everyone 12

everything 12

except 12

F

faculty 13

fail 4

family 3

finish 4

for 32, 1, 8

for + time 3

forbid 4

forget 4

G

gerund 4

get through 4

group 11

H

had better 5

had + infinitive 5

had + past participle 2

have + past participle 2

herself 27

himself 27

hope 4

how 14

I

if 14

in 32

in the last few days 3

indefinite article 31

indefinite subject 12

indirect speech 5

infinitive 4

intend 4

into 32

itself 27

J

just 3

K

keep 4

keep on 4

L

lately 3

learn 4

less...than 10

like 10

look forward to 4

M

majority 13

many 25

may 5

mean 4

might 5

misplaced modifier 7

modal verbs 5

modals 5

more than 30, 10

most 30

must 5

myself 27

N

neither 12

neither...nor 9

no one 12

nor 8

not only...but also 9

nothing 12

noun 25

noun clause 14

noun clause connector 14

noun clause connector/object 16

noun clause connector/subject 15

O

object of prepositions 4

object of verbs 4

of 32

offer 4

on 32

one 25

one of the 30

or 8

orchestra 3

ought (to) 5

ourselves 27

over 32

P

parallel structure 8, 9, 10

participle 4

passive meaning 4

passive voice 24

past participle 5

past perfect tense 2

past tense 1

personal pronoun 26

plan 4

plan on 4

plural noun 25

police 3

possessive pronoun 26

postpone 4

practice 4

preposition 32

present perfect tense 1, 2

pretend 4

pronoun 26

pronoun reference 28

public 13

put off 4

R

recently 3

reflexive pronoun 26, 27

refuse 4

relative adverb 17

relative clause marker 16

relative pronoun 17

S

series 13

several 25

shall 5

should 5

similar to 10

since 1, 3

single 25

singular noun 25

so far 3

so...that 21

some 12

staff 13

stop 4

subject-verb agreement 11, 12, 13

subject of verb 4

subject with appositive 11

subjunctive mood (conditionals) 22, 23

such...that 21

suggest 4

superlatives 30

superlative degree 30

T

team 13

than 10

that 14, 16, 18

the 31

the most 30

the rest 12

the same as 10

themselves 27

think about 4

think of 4

time adverbs 3

time expressions 3

time markers 1

to 32

toward 32

two 25

two, three, four dollars 13

two, three, four miles 13

V

variety 13

various 25

verb phrases 4

verbals 4

W

what 7, 12

whatever 7, 12

when 12, 15, 16

whenever 12

where 14, 17, 18

wherever 14

whether 14

whether...or 9

which 16, 18

who 15, 16, 18

whoever 12, 18

whom 16, 18

whose 16, 18

why 14

will 5

with 32

would 5

Y

yet 1, 3, 8

yourself 27

yourselves 27

ACKNOWLEDGMENTS

The author would like to thank his colleagues and students for their invaluable assistance in bringing this book to life.

The author and publisher are grateful to those who have made this publication possible by providing all kinds of support from editing, graphic design, and proof-reading. Efforts have been made to identify the source of materials used in this book; however, it has not always been possible to identify the sources of all the materials used, or to trace the copyright holders. If any omissions are brought to our attention, we will be happy to include the appropriate acknowledgements on reprinting.

ABOUT THE AUTHOR

Richard Lee is a professor of English and distinguished publishing scholar with numerous books published under his name. His books are available on Amazon, other online stores, and in bookstores worldwide. He pursued his doctoral education at the University of Rochester in New York and the University of British Columbia and received his Ph.D. in English.

www.ingramcontent.com/pod-product-compliance
Lightning Source LLC
Chambersburg PA
CBHW071849230426
43671CB00012B/2123